ALL MEN ARE ASSHOLES

(... AND ALL WOMEN ARE CRAZY)

ALL MEN ARE ASSHOLES

(... AND ALL WOMEN ARE CRAZY)

A lesson on how to find love
when everyone is awful

by

JORDAN WEST

West Press

Disclaimer:

I have changed certain names and modified identifying features, including dialogue, locations and physical descriptions of individuals to preserve anonymity and avoid losing a bar fight. In some cases composite characters have been created or timelines have been compressed in order to further preserve privacy and to maintain narrative flow. Any celebrity mention is merely a fabrication of my disturbing imagination or unpopular personal opinion and in no way reflects factual information or events. It's only satire, people. The intention was to protect everyone's privacy and reputations (except my own) without damaging the integrity of the story. Though it is safe to say that my personal integrity has become a casualty.

Published by West Press

Print ISBN 978-1-9851-3664-9

Typesetting services by BOOKOW.COM

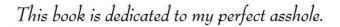

This book is dedicated to my perfect asshole.

CONTENTS

INTRODUCTION

"I was glad I wasn't in love, that I wasn't happy with the world. I like being at odds with everything. People in love often become edgy, dangerous. They lose their sense of perspective. They lose their sense of humor. They become nervous, psychotic bores. They even become killers."

—Charles Bukowski, *Women*

L IFE is a fickle bitch.

We have all been placed on this earth for one purpose: evolution. That's it. Your life, after death, means nothing.

Take a moment to let that sink in.

We come into this world the same way—bawling, covered in the placenta and blood that's clung to our shriveled skin after making the long, claustrophobic journey through our mother's birth canal, only to spit out of an unshaven vagina, straight into the hands of a masked stranger. If you're sitting there and thinking, "Well actually, I was a C-section baby," you should probably just forget about reading this book because nothing I have to say could possibly pertain to someone as unique and special as you, Snow Leopard.

After birth, it's up to your parents to screw you up just enough so that you're hurdled into adulthood with confusion and uncertainty, eventually leaving them to blame for all your busted dreams. Once you fly the coop, you'll probably spend years coasting through life collecting debt and bad habits before accidentally slipping into parenthood yourself.

You'll enjoy a few months obsessing over your new addition and littering social media with the same photos day in and day out, annoying everyone around you. Then you'll take a couple years adding mouths to feed to avoid the guilt of raising an only child. You'll eventually experience some form of parental disdain, which basically amounts to never admitting the regret you feel towards having children but secretly dreaming about all the cool shit you probably would have done had it not been for parenthood.

Finally, when you start to grow old, you will come to terms with it all, grateful for the experiences you've carved out of life, and then eventually you will die. Just like that. Just like everyone else. And in the end, you get to stick your kids with a funeral bill for any trouble they might have caused you along the way—life's little Whoopee cushion.

And so goes the circle of life. Okay, maybe this is the worst-case scenario. Maybe for you, procreation is the greatest gift of all, and your contribution to humanity is the pinnacle of your existence.

Now, at some point along this seemingly long, but undeniably short path we're paving to the grave, love comes along—likely more than once—and this crazy, fucked-up thing we spend our entire lives obsessing over sort of makes it all worth it. Somehow.

What you eventually learn about love is that while it has its intermittent moments of passion and fulfillment, it's mostly one cruel son of a bitch. Love is that torturous emo tune your heartstrings write. It's the reason people get out of bed every day and keep on sucking life's dick.

Love sends you over the edge into a whirlwind of madness, to the very brink of insanity. And while most people never quite make it to a padded room bound by a straitjacket, we will all come very, very close. If you can confidently say you've never wanted to light a match and set someone's car on fire, you're probably just a very a good liar. Life is one thing, but love, now, that's a whole other sad bastard. While we may have only been put on this earth for human evolution, there is a task at hand: learning how to find a love worth keeping and, in that process, finding a self worth loving.

* * *

Love is a fickler bitch.

In all likelihood, The One is just a well-executed prank by Hallmark's marketing team, and yet if science would allow it, we would spend an eternity searching for that person. On the other hand, maybe The One does exist, and if they do, I would imagine that they probably find you at your least desirable, when you're too confused, crazy or corrupted to even realize they're standing behind you in line at Whole Foods, clutching overpriced avocados. If you feel like you're one of the few who has found your one true love, contact me in 20 years, because I would love to hear about how that's working out.

I'm not some kind of relationship nihilist who doesn't believe in the idea of true love, I just don't think it's necessarily in everyone's cards. Some people find love and others eat shit and die; it all depends on the gambles you take with the hand you're dealt.

Eventually, most people will find someone like-minded, someone who faces the toilet paper the same way and doesn't mind the way you kind of smell like a musty bathmat in the morning, but that person probably wasn't specifically set on this earth by a higher power to find you and then make your life better. And sure, it always seems like destiny in the beginning, but after few years spent smelling each other's farts and pretending not to be bothered by their annoying eating habits, you'll come to realize that, like the generations before you and before them, you've probably just found someone you're able to coexist with.

The exciting part of love is the challenging journey you embark on as you make your way through life towards that special bore you eventually decide to settle down with. The explosive crazies and the impenetrable assholes you get the pleasure of encountering along the way are the people who eventually fuck you up so badly that if The One did happen to cross your path, they probably wouldn't want you. Very few people are lucky enough to encounter their perfect mate when the timing is right. And yet so many people proclaim to have met their soul mate.

These people are idiots.

Do you know who also claimed to be soul mates? Paul Bernardo and Karla Homolka. While I'm sure they loved each other (and nothing really says true love like collectively raping and murdering three teenage girls), perhaps the term "soul mate" was a little impetuous here.

* * *

Paul Bernardo reportedly raped 19 women before he even met Karla. While it's not proven, he's presumed to be the Scarborough Rapist. He admitted to raping all three murdered women, but he insisted it was Karla who killed them. All 19 previous rape victims are still alive. To this day, the true story is still at large. One thing I do know is that Karla Homolka is a free woman, while Paul Bernardo remains behind bars in maximum security. You mean to tell me that maybe, just maybe, after watching her new husband repeatedly have sex with other women, it's not even remotely possible that this might have catapulted Karla Homolka into a homicidal rage? Maybe the intention never was murder. Maybe the terms rape and open relationship were grey areas for them?

Take a minute and just go here with me.

I would imagine if this were the case, the turmoil and scandal became too much for Karla to emotionally handle. Eventually, she freaked out, smashed some cheap dishes they were gifted at their wedding and let out grotesque howls of anger before lunging to a death grasp. The first time it was an accident, and the second and third would have happened naturally, as death is a permanent solution to any problem.

Once they were found out, Paul was prepared to sink with the ship, while crazy Karla switched into survival mode. She insisted that Paul made her do all that murderin'. He made her crazy. He pushed her to insanity. Karla decided—after being heavily influenced by her attorney —that she was abused to the point of submission. Right?

Doubtful. Karla is calculated and manipulative and, like anyone, she probably realized that a life behind bars wasn't exactly what she had in mind for the next 65 years. Karla knew it was survival of the fittest, so she drowned Paul to save herself. (This scenario is a complete fabrication of my imagination. Whether any of it holds true, I have no idea. It's important to sound like you know what you're talking about when you're writing a book.)

Paul Bernardo is an asshole. The supreme asshole of assholes. He deserves every agonizing minute he spends imagining life on the outside while receiving an anal-pillaging by some tattooed, bitch-making prison bear, because such is the fate of a supreme asshole—though he's probably in protective, one can dream. But Karla Homolka is far from innocent. Karla is crazy. Batshit, motherfucking crazy, and she's out there roaming the streets, probably stopping by the grocery store to pick up cereal and salad dressing on her way home from some God-awful telemarketing job. Crazy Karla Homolka is likely among the slew of insufferable bloodsuckers that call you at the worst times to ask if you'd like to participate in a survey about your cable service while her ex-husband spends an eternity trading blowjobs for cigarettes.

Paul Bernardo is an asshole and Karla Homolka is crazy, and these are two people who claimed to have found true love. The only thing that separates you from the "Ken and Barbie Killers" is that you're (probably) not a psychopath.

This uplifting trip down memory lane brings me full circle. To finding love or, well, at least avoiding a felony.

All men are assholes. Not necessarily to the degree of Paul Bernardo, but all men exercise their inner asshole on a daily basis. It's their defense mechanism. Men will spend their entire adulthood searching for the perfect Martha Stewart level of crazy that they are able to coexist and procreate with. Meanwhile, they will screw everything with legs and a heartbeat until they find it. All men know this, and any man will admit it.

On the flip side, all women are completely and unapologetically out of their goddamn minds. As a woman, I can wholeheartedly promise you that we are all totally and absolutely crazy. Women obsess over finding love with that perfect prince charming that possesses all the qualities they require for procreation. Women will lie, cheat and steal to attain the love they feel they deserve. Most women don't know this, and those who do will certainly deny it.

While the ultimate goal for a man is to find that low-level lunatic he can learn to live with, the ultimate goal for a woman is to find that one special asshole that doesn't make her any crazier than she already is.

And this is what we call a revelation. Or a theme worthy of two hundred pages. Whatever.

CRAZY SCALE

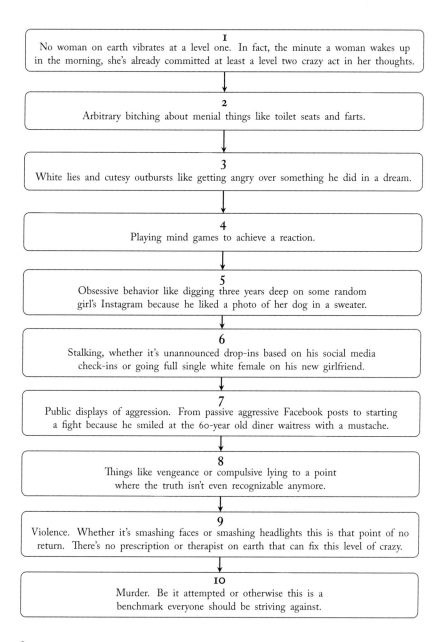

1
No woman on earth vibrates at a level one. In fact, the minute a woman wakes up in the morning, she's already committed at least a level two crazy act in her thoughts.

2
Arbitrary bitching about menial things like toilet seats and farts.

3
White lies and cutesy outbursts like getting angry over something he did in a dream.

4
Playing mind games to achieve a reaction.

5
Obsessive behavior like digging three years deep on some random girl's Instagram because he liked a photo of her dog in a sweater.

6
Stalking, whether it's unannounced drop-ins based on his social media check-ins or going full single white female on his new girlfriend.

7
Public displays of aggression. From passive aggressive Facebook posts to starting a fight because he smiled at the 60-year old diner waitress with a mustache.

8
Things like vengeance or compulsive lying to a point where the truth isn't even recognizable anymore.

9
Violence. Whether it's smashing faces or smashing headlights this is that point of no return. There's no prescription or therapist on earth that can fix this level of crazy.

10
Murder. Be it attempted or otherwise this is a benchmark everyone should be striving against.

ASSHOLE SCALE

1
Similar to women and the crazy scale, no man is a level one asshole. If you think you know someone who is, capture him, cage him and donate him to science. Or just leave him where you've already put him: in the friend zone.

2
Constantly correcting people. Feeling compelled to let others know you're smarter than they are is just annoying.

3
Ghosting. It's a really great way for a man to find out just how crazy a woman can be without actually getting to know her.

4
Aggressive unwarranted flirting. Learning to take a hint isn't easy, but there's a good chance that unsolicited dick pic is getting a lot of laughs from every person she encounters in the following 72 hours.

5
Narcissism. Flaunting an ego around–be it money, looks or brains– is impossible to look past. These people are grade A douchebags.

6
Leading someone on, whether it's for personal gratification or to avoid hurting her feelings, is probably going to land him an arsenal of whiny, novel-length texts and emails about how much he doesn't deserve her.

7
Manipulation. From petty comments or insults to full-blown gaslighting, seeking control of a person is only a testament to one's own insecurities.

8
Infidelity. It's probably the quickest way to wake up one morning with words like CHEATER and SCUMBAG smeared all over your car in feces.

9
Violence. Hitting people is wrong. But men who hit women are exceptions to that rule.

10
Murder. Be it attempted or otherwise this is a benchmark everyone should be striving against.

CHAPTER 1:
THE BASTARD

"Fatherhood is great because you can ruin someone from scratch."

—Jon Stewart

I don't have daddy issues.

Okay, so just because I've never met my biological father, and just because I've had the misfortune of watching my mother sink herself in multiple relationships before I even hit puberty, doesn't mean I've been bred for mental instability when it comes to men. It really doesn't.

At least I'm pretty sure it doesn't. However, let's rewind for a minute because the series of unfortunate boyfriends and my climb to the top of the crazy tree wouldn't be complete without a little backstory.

This can of worms begins in 1991, on the day I heard the phrase, "Honey, you're a bastard." My late grandmother really had a way with words. As you can imagine, this was somewhat traumatic for a five-year-old who still believed that she could force the rain to stop by singing the "Mister Sun" song. However, similar to the devastating blow you experience when you learn that professional wrestling isn't real and world peace is nothing but folk singer's pipe dream, I eventually got over it.

My mother was always a vivacious woman. The type whom sad, despondent men write poems and songs about. She grew up with three older brothers, so when she wasn't crying to get her way, she was being tortured and picked on. At a pretty young age, my mother learned how to stand up for herself and fight back. This is probably the reason she's been married three times. And also the reason she's managed to bounce back from every failed relationship without so much as a scratch. I'm confident my mother aspired to be Elizabeth Taylor at one point or another.

One thing I'm certain of: despite the number of hearts she's broken, I've caught her crying on the kitchen floor into a tub of ice cream enough times to realize that no matter how hard you work to overcome the obstacles in your relationships, nothing is guaranteed because people can change. Absolutely nothing in this life is owed to you and love is sure to be the one thing that makes you aware of that. My mother, the eternal lover and unfortunate repeat offender, was always my greatest teacher.

* * *

My mother was working at the hospital in the laundry department when she met Max. After giving birth to me while living in a women's shelter, she quickly had to find a job to support us. But like any single new mother, she also knew that the quickest way out of her single-parent hardship was to find herself a husband to carry the brunt of the financial load. No one really had morals in the '80s, so this was hardly even considered shallow. From there it was only a hop, skip and a two-year jump before she and Max were married. He was a bonafide badass who rode a motorcycle and ran with a nefarious crew. One year after their wedding, she gave birth to my brother. And after an expectedly tumultuous three-year marriage, they signed the divorce papers.

It was probably for the best. At the time, Max was an alcoholic. I remember sitting at the top of the stairs in our little condo, consoling my brother while we watched them throw fists and obscenities at each other in the living room. Max was an angry man and my mother was too independent to let that hinder her. However, a few years after splitting from her, Max turned a new leaf. He chopped off his mullet and joined a congregation. Now he's a reverend who travels to Africa as a missionary, helping orphanages. Who says God can't change people?

Determined to make a better life for herself, my mother enrolled in college. Then after graduating from law and security administration, she applied to the RCMP. As my impending teenage misfortune would have it, she was accepted. But with admittance, came a required six-month training period in Saskatchewan. At this time, we were shacked up with my mother's new boyfriend, Neil. Neil was a seven-foot giant who'd lost his basketball scholarship to a knee injury and an opioid addiction.

I'd just turned five and was quickly learning about all kinds of weird shit that a five-year-old probably shouldn't be subjected to. Like the afternoon I pressed play on Neil's VCR, assuming *ET* was still in the player, and a slutty nurse with a mouthful of balls appeared on the TV screen instead of my beloved alien.

I can't be entirely sure why, but when my mother took off for training, I was left under Neil's supervision. Maybe he was deemed trustworthy? But the most likely scenario is that it was just an inconvenience to call my school and change my bus route.

Parenting in the '80s was subpar. If you were born between the years of 1979 and 1989, you were probably nothing more than a social experiment. Our folks wanted the best for us by exerting the least amount of effort. They would tell us we were special and could achieve ridiculously high standards if we just believed in ourselves, all while chain-smoking in an unventilated apartment with a pet boa constrictor on the coffee table. The '80s were basically just a maelstrom of bad hair and irresponsible parenting.

I remember after a couple of weeks with Neil, I was ready for a change of scenery. I wanted to go somewhere that I was cared for and coddled like a new pet puppy. I wanted to go to a place that was free of rules and had an endless collection of old crap covered in moth-balls to snoop through. A place I was appreciated for being a weird little creep who wanted to be left alone to contort my Barbies into the awkward sex positions I'd seen in that porno. I wanted to go to my grandmother's house.

My grandmother was a strange bird. Her intentions were always sincere, but, as I've established, she had a flair for drama. If you've never seen the movie *Running With Scissors*, you're missing out on a performance by Annette Benning that is not only flawless but probably a better comparison to my grandmother than I am capable of expressing.

Her entire house was decorated in white ducks. There wasn't a single wall that escaped her penchant for the odd waterfowl. This isn't an exaggeration. Her obsession was borderline compulsive. Every morning, she would take me up the road to the creek along the railroad tracks to feed the ducks and watch the trains go by. Once in a while she'd convince me to scale the bank of the creek and trudge through the pond to pick a few of the sausage-like cattails for her. We spent the weekends roaming shopping malls, getting our hair done and raiding yard sale after yard sale in search of more duck memorabilia. My grandmother was the type of woman who took photographs of photographs, as if living in constant fear that she might lose the image. There's probably a diagnosis for this.

We watched a lot of TV together. Her bunny-eared television set only had three programs as far as I was concerned: CMT's video countdown, the Shopping Channel, and *America's Most Wanted* (however, in 1994 the OJ Simpson trial became a strong fourth). She would tell me horror stories about children that had gone missing and how their bodies were discovered in the woods, bound to a tree with tarp straps after being pecked and clawed to an unrecognizable death. I spent my entire childhood petrified of crowded spaces, worried that I would be kidnapped. I never wanted to go to Disneyland because the probability of being abducted by a sex pervert haunted my ability to enjoy anything adventurous. Thanks to my grandmother's affinity for crime shows and CNN newscasts in the '90s, I went to bed every night fearful that Michael Jackson was under my bed.

As she entered old age, her body began to give out and she eventually had part of her bowel removed. This resulted in a stoma and the attachment of a colostomy bag to her abdomen. I made the dreadful mistake of telling my grandmother that I wanted to be a doctor one day, so she insisted that I learn how to change her creepy poo bag.

Don't even talk to me about your childhood traumas.

This procedure kicked off a whole slew of doctor's visits and operations. Phone calls to my grandmother became biology lessons. She was periodically bedridden for months at a time with an IV attached to her bedside. She purchased a hospital bed to replace the one in her bedroom so that she could be wheeled into the living room and then sit up at the push of a button to watch all the TV programs that tormented me.

This was the catalyst for her Sears addiction. Every week, I'd have a new package waiting for me after school, something she ordered from the Sears catalogue. Usually some ridiculous outfit I hated. I was a tomboy, but she was always forcing me into dresses and floral prints. I was wrangled into modeling each and every heinous ensemble while she smiled from her hospital bed and my grandfather took pictures. Photographs she would probably later take photographs of once they were developed.

This sounds like the type of thing that happens in a pedophile's basement. It wasn't.

Back to the bastard thing.

One Friday just after lunch, my grandmother showed up to my elementary school in a green floral summer dress, clutching a dismissal slip. She handed the small yellow piece of paper to my teacher and told me to collect my things. Her makeup was flawless behind her coke-bottle lenses, and not a hair in her red perm stood out of place. As she swept me from the classroom, she informed me that she had set up a photo shoot for us that afternoon. My grandmother tied my hair into a sleek ponytail before we got into the car and raced to the mall. When we entered the department store, she instructed me to pick out a blue dress. She insisted on the color to match my blue eyes, as she was wearing green because her eyes were green. This made perfect sense for someone who did most of her shopping from a mechanical hospital bed in her living room.

We decided on this God-awful, blue floral, lace-trimmed number because it was the perfect child-sized replica of the one she was wearing. My grandmother ripped off the tag and made her way to the checkout to pay for the dress as I used the fitting room to change into it. Whether she actually paid for that dress or not will always remain a mystery to me. Not because my grandmother was poor, but because she was just that insane.

Later that night, we sat on her porch drinking tea in our fancy photo shoot dresses. My grandmother regaled me with exaggerated stories from her childhood as she smoked cigarettes. Meanwhile, a Popeye's candy stick slung from my lip, mimicking her habit.

Suddenly, my grandmother arched her back and sat up as if she were struck by a muscle spasm. She turned to me with a sinister glint in her eye, "Jordan, it's important you always know the truth. I know a secret, would you like to know what it is?" she toyed.

I nodded curiously, plucking the candy stick from my lips with my index and middle finger as I pretended to exhale smoke from my candy cigarette.

She hesitated for a minute, watching me. But before she could reconsider her madness, she blurted, "Honey, you're a bastard. Max is not your real father. He's Sterling's father, but he's not yours."

I stared back at her for a few moments before I could muster words, "What do you mean?"

Because Max had been around for as long as I could remember, I'd been brought up with the understanding that he was my dad too.

"You and Sterling have different fathers. Your mother met Max after you were born so he can't be your biological father." She stopped, realizing she was talking to a five-year-old and corrected herself, "Biological means real. Do you understand?"

"I guess so. If Max isn't my dad, who is then?"

"Your mother isn't certain."

"Oh," I replied as my eyes began to well with tears. I stared at my grandmother as she continued to smoke her cancer stick and sip her tea. She picked up the paper on the side table and began to flip through it. I don't know if she had mixed up her medication that day or maybe her poo bag had backflowed all the way to her brain, but I often wonder if my sweet grandmother was in fact a sociopath. "I want to call my mom." I quivered.

I began to cry as soon as my mother picked up the phone. I explained to her what my grandmother had told me and asked if it were true.

She calmly responded, "Nana is telling you the truth, but it doesn't change anything. Max loves you just the same. I promise we'll talk about it when I get home. Until then, don't worry about any of that. I love you. Now please put Nana on the phone."

I turned the phone over to our Judas and before she could even say "Hello," I heard my mother scream through the receiver. My grandmother walked into the other room, dragging the obnoxiously long curly cord behind her.

I still have the tiny photo of my grandmother and me in our matching floral dresses. It's propped up on my vanity in a little gold frame, right next to a portrait of Julius and Ethel Rosenberg.

I guess you could say things changed after that. I was overcome with a strange insecurity and an overall feeling of loss but between Max and Neil, I had plenty of father figures to go around.

There are worse things than finding out you're a bastard. Like, finding out you're one of the king's bastards and that the monarchy would want you dead if they knew so you're sent to The Wall where it perpetually snows and everyone smells like BO. Or finding out that your biological father is some kind of colossal fuckup like Gary Ridgeway or Corey Feldman. I'm just saying, it probably could have been worse.

Three weeks later, my grandmother told me there wasn't a Santa Claus. I honestly don't know which unwarranted confession was more traumatic. The '90s were a soulless and cruel time.

* * *

In 1993, when my mother graduated from the RCMP training program, we were posted in Quesnel BC, the turd-cutter of Western Canada. The town smells like rotten egg farts 12 months a year. What's more horrifying is that you eventually get used to it. Nobody there has any idea what it's like to live outside of a Dutch oven. Neil knew an opportunity when he saw one, so he tagged along and got a job teaching at the local high school.

After about a year, Neil started showing signs of violence, mostly with my brother. I remember one day, while my mother was at work, I came around the corner into the hallway and he had his enormous hand clasped around my brother's throat as his little body dangled in the air against the wall. Sterling had accidentally let Neil's two German Shepherds out of the back yard when he came home from school without double-checking the latch. When Neil spotted me standing at the end of the hallway, he dropped my brother. I watched as guilt consumed his rage. Sterling took a lot of heat from him but we never told my mother about it.

One afternoon, my mother and Neil picked us up from school because a blizzard had rendered the school busses out of commission. When we pulled into the driveway, we could hear the dogs barking from inside the garage where Neil kept them during the cold months. I looked over to the giant as he shifted the truck into park. The twinkle of fury in his eyes was unmistakable. He panted heavily before he stepped out of the vehicle, walked over the garage, and opened the door. We watched in horror from the bench seat in the truck. My mother knew he had lost his mind. He swung at one of the German Shepherds, but the dog moved just before Neil's open palm could connect with his muzzle. He screamed feverishly at them as their defensive barks grew louder. Finally, he grabbed each canine by the collar, and with superhero strength, picked both full-grown German Shepherds off their feet, choking the life from them. He carried the dogs across the garage, set them down, opened the back door to the yard and aggressively threw them out into the snow, one by one.

My brother began to cry as he looked on in fear. He loved those dogs. They whimpered away from Neil, sore and confused. The three of us scurried out of the truck and into the house. My mother quickly led us into her bedroom. We sat on the bed behind the closed the door and she wrapped my distraught brother in her arms. She looked at me as I sat frozen and torn between fear and familiar sadness. She realized there was a pattern forming and it was time to pull the chute.

We moved out a few weeks later.

It was probably for the best. Not too long after that, one of Neil's students charged him with sexual assault. He was fired and forced to move back to Ontario where he's likely living in his mother's basement, chatting on the Internet with some fat, bald Russian catfish as he reminisces about that time he almost leeched his way to something better. (Note: I recently received a text from my mother that read: *"Ding-dong the witch is dead."* As it turns out, Neil died of cancer. And my mother has zero chill.)

* * *

During the time my mother was with Neil, she made friends with another Mountie, Will. Conveniently, Will and his longtime girlfriend split up around the same time we'd become homeless so my mother rented a dilapidated three-bedroom apartment across town as a makeshift place to call home while she sparked a well-timed romance with Will. He was posted in a small town about an hour away, Wells BC, population: 100. He was the only cop in town so the Force paid for his housing and that basically made him a celebrity. Just to be clear, Will wasn't a Jedi and this book isn't about to take a nerd-turn. The Force is how other Mounties refer to the police academy.

We spent my mother's days off in Wells, dirt-biking, hiking, and fishing in the summer. When winter rolled around, we took on sledding and snowmobiling. Will was a lot of fun, but I was always a little skeptical of his decorative choices. He hung his skis above his TV in the living room and his bicycle was mounted to the wall next to the dining room table. Nothing seemed right about that. But he quickly redeemed himself when he taught me how to cheat in Super Mario Bros.

I'd stay with him while my mother worked nights. He helped me build space shuttles and time machines out of the wardrobe boxes in his spare bedroom and let me use his waterbed to practice pole-jump landings. Will was a big kid, he was cool and we bonded over shit like wiping out on quads, horror movies, and sneaking onto old mining farms to pan for gold. I was basically the son (accomplice) he always wanted. I couldn't have been happier when he asked my mother to marry him.

One night, we were on the couch, watching *Nightmare on Elm Street.* I looked over to Will, and with every inch of 10-year-old awkwardness I could muster I blurted: "I think I want you to be my dad." Fighting back tears, he pressed his lips together and passed me the popcorn. I reached into the bowl for a handful and turned back to the TV. From that day forward Will became Dad.

They were married in June of 1996 and immediately put in for a transfer to Vancouver Island, desperate for a simple life with neutral smells. My brother and I were shipped to Ontario where we would spend a couple months with family while Will and my mother searched for a home in paradise.

* * *

I will never forget the warm July afternoon my mother picked me up from the airport in Nanaimo. When I stepped out of the plane and onto the tarmac, a warm, unfamiliar draft of West Coast breeze flirted against my skin. It was exciting, foreign, and smelled nothing like flatulence.

We drove along the old highway in my dad's convertible Fiat with the roof down. With the ocean to our left and the sun behind the mountainous terrain on the right creating breaks of shade and shapes along the pavement, we felt like we were in a movie. That cliché scene at the end of a long drama where the protagonist drives off into the sunset with their dog and the credits begin to roll.

Ladysmith was a strange town, a real-world *Pleasantville.* It was a community of eager-greeters. Everyone knew your name and everyone wanted to know your business. We'd started in a place where the only thing you could see for miles was concrete and power lines—and I guess we made a pit stop in a giant shart—but we'd finally landed in this picturesque suburbia with cookie-cutter lawns that the men all seemed to mow at the same time while waving to each other shirtless. They threw block parties and neighborhood BBQ's. The women got together and drank wine while gossiping about whoever declined their invite. I was convinced we'd gotten messed up in some kind of WACO shit because this level of contentment and social obligation wasn't normal.

Needless to say, it wasn't difficult making friends in Ladysmith. Everyone was delighted to meet the new cop-couple on the block. I think my parents granted the neighbors a sense of security. From what exactly, I have no idea. Probably each other, bunch of Ted Bundys.

Life, as you can imagine, was pretty simple. I started grade five in the fall and was once again the new girl with the boy's name. But after the utter hilarity of that dissipated(eyeroll), kids warmed up to me. I eventually found myself surrounded by the popular crowd. I was smart and cynical, which I guess was confusing for a bunch of prepubescent kids because for some reason they elected me as their student class president in grade school. The most important thing I did during my tyrannical reign was get a pop machine installed in the cafeteria, which conveniently, was the only thing I promised in my nomination speech. If I were American, I would run for president based solely on my success rate. I'm not. And Canadian politics barely matter so I guess I'll stick to hoping I can sell this book.

The years flew and I'd never seen my mother so content. They were grossly in love. The passion in their marriage was effortless and something to be envied. By other gross adults. I remember asking them to walk a few steps behind me at the movies because they were holding hands. No one else's parents were as publicly humiliating as mine but I guess it could have been worse.

In the fall of 2001, I was 15 and my mother suggested I get an afterschool job. They thought it would teach me the value in saving and earning the things you wanted in life. I thought it was a great way to afford my newfound weekend drinking habit. So I began my short-lived burger-flipping career at McDonald's. I took the job there for the same reason anyone takes a job at McDonald's, because you're completely unfit to work anywhere else that requires a social security number.

The owners, Ned and Heather, were a fun-loving married couple and they really hit it off with my folks. Their friendship evolved quickly.

From dinner parties, to shopping, to vacations, they did everything together. My mother genuinely appreciated her friendship with Heather. They swapped clothing and exchanged secrets. My dad spent his afternoons golfing with Ned or playing pool at the local pub. Around this time, my parents decided to turn our family room into a bar. Every day I'd come home from school to find Heather and my mom drinking wine and smoking cigarettes in that room while they planned their next escapade.

So there we were, the perfect family and the perfect home, with the perfect life, in the perfect neighborhood, right on top of Bullshit Mountain.

* * *

Around grade 11, my parents started to get into minor arguments that eventually escalated into screaming matches. I had no idea what they were even fighting over, but it seemed influenced. My mother would confide in Heather, and Heather always reacted to her relationship woes with concern and empathy.

One weekend, my mother fled to Vancouver on an RCMP training course (they were required to take a few each year). She left in a heated feud with my dad, completely unaware of the turmoil about to unfold.

The following night, I came home from a party drunk and stoned. I didn't turn on any lights when I came home in fear of waking up my dad. I continued with my usual wasted routine where I would forage through the fridge for snacks, while drinking orange juice from the carton. Just then, I spotted movement in my peripheral. Naturally, I looked away from the illuminated icebox, through the kitchen window toward the back deck. I noticed the hot tub was uncovered and the light was on. I curiously moved closer to the window to get a better look. The glare from the stove light was distracting my view outside so I cupped my temples as I pressed my forehead against the window. It took a few seconds to focus my bloodshot eyes. Once everything came into focus, I gasped and stumbled backwards, knocking over a chair at the table. The crash was heard from outside because all three adults stopped what they were doing and sprung to attention. My dad was horrified. He sobered instantly as he awkwardly jumped out of the hot tub and came rushing for the back door.

I had caught my dad red-handed, making out with a topless Heather in our hot tub while one of their friends drunkenly sat back completely unfazed sipping his beer. I turned and ran towards my room, slamming the door behind me. He didn't follow after me.

When something like this happens to you, it's as if the world pauses for a moment to allow your entire life to flash before your eyes. Everything you're led to believe comes raging down in an avalanche of beastly destruction and broken promises. And then you realize you're drunk and it's probably all just a figment of your imagination.

Sunday morning, I woke up and left the house. I didn't return home until the following night when my mom returned from the city.

I stormed through the front door Monday evening, prepared to tell her everything. To my dismay, I had crashed my dad's confessional. He knew my relationship with my mother was seamless. Our relationship goes deeper than picking sides. She was the only constant in my life and my loyalty would always be with her.

They both had tears in their eyes as I boomed into the living room. I looked at my mother with complete sorrow before my gaze shifted to my dad. He shamefully looked away as I blinked at him in disbelief. I decided to say nothing. Instead, I slinked off to my room and waited for my mother.

An hour later, my bedroom door creaked open and my mother peered in from the hallway, "Can I come in?"

I nodded. She moved toward my bed, reaching for the remote to turn off the TV. I looked up at her tear-soaked face and she started to cry again.

"Are you ok?" I asked.

"I will be," she responded as she crawled into the bed next to me and curled up to go to sleep.

"What's next?" I stared at her, unsure which answer I wanted to hear.

"I just. I don't know yet. This shouldn't have happened and I'm sorry." With that, she fell asleep.

My dad moved out the following week.

He is still the person I call my father. Our bond never faded and I love him for carrying that role when he really didn't have to. But their separation was probably for the best. My dad is the ultimate bachelor and he's now free to hang his athletic gear on the wall of his living room in lieu of art.

* * *

My mother went on to date the owner of a local coffee shop. They quickly moved in and then quickly broke up as he lacked an ability to show excitement over anything. Ben was intelligent and intriguing and initially my mother was drawn to his mystery. He was well read and completely different than anyone she'd ever dated. He liked expensive wine, Tori Amos, and reading poetry. But Ben was lazy. His car was a rolling episode of hoarders. He was a kept man and that worked for him, but eventually it drove my mother to drink.

One night we cornered her in the kitchen and improvised an intervention. She knew she had a problem. She broke down and a week later she left Ben.

It was probably for the best as Ben had a traveling heart. He wound up selling the coffee shop and jet setting around the world. And let's be honest, only assholes take poetry seriously.

* * *

After Ben, my mother moved on to an ex-boxer who seemed sweet and kind at first. But in the end, a boxer knows only one solution and it's found in the weight behind his fists.

Glen was a man you could tell used to be very handsome. Unfortunately, all the blows to the head left him with a lazy eye and a nonexistent attention span. He followed my mother to Ontario when she put in for a transfer. Everything started out well, but Glen turned. One night he came home drunk and took a swing at her. Luckily, my mother was trained in drunk douchebag combat, so she got away un-scathed. She left him too and followed with a restraining order that had him exiled from the province.

It was probably for the best. I can't imagine what life would have been like for an ex-boxer like Glen, perpetually losing fights to a girl.

* * *

My mother has recently been remarried and to a much younger man. Danny is even-tempered, with all the right intentions and to really shake things up, he has more than one syllable in his name. They own a pool and I guess in Eastern Canada if you can say you own a pool, you've made it.

Her new husband is younger than my current boyfriend. I don't know what that says about her. Or me.

Okay, so maybe I have daddy issues.

CHAPTER 1.5:
RESILIENCE

"Insanity is doing the same thing over and over again and expecting different results."

—Albert Einstein (or some idiot on the internet falsely
accrediting quotes.)

Y mother's romantic escapades were the mold for my adulthood. What I managed to take from her is that no matter how great a lover or a fighter you may be, you are no match for the wrath of loss. And sometimes losing means dragging ass through the trenches of muddy despair to find the shower of salvation.

Woody Allen is a perfect example of someone who completely lost the plot—and I mean that's pretty incredible for someone who's made a career out of creating plots. I guess he missed the Please Do Not Fuck label that came tagged to step-fatherhood. (Maybe it was in the fine print. No one ever reads that shit.)

Here we have an older man, in a 12-year relationship with a young and talented Mia Farrow. But she came with baggage from her previous marriage. Five children, two of whom were adopted.

One day an unsuspecting Mia stumbles across nude photos of her appallingly unattractive adopted daughter in her boyfriend's sock drawer. I doubt looks mattered in the grand scheme of things, but it's worth the mention. Soon Yi is not some hot piece of ass. She probably called Woody Dad at this point, which paints a very uncomfortable picture of their current sex-life.

He eventually marries her because everyone knows that marriage is a really effective way of sweeping creepiness under the rug. Then they danced into the horizon, happily ever after. To the chorus from Time of the Season by The Zombies. This is probably not true, but the image is totally hilarious. It's fair to say, Woody Allen probably wasn't given any World's Best Dad coffee mugs that Christmas.

He and Soon Yi have since adopted more children. I'm sorry, what? Clearly there was absolutely no lesson learned here. No one plays against the odds like Soon Yi. No one.

Lessons worth learning come few and far between, I guess.

Meanwhile, back at the ranch, poor Mia was left defeated and broken with the rest of the brood. The eight children Woody wasn't attracted to. Well, the seven he wasn't attracted to and the one he allegedly sexually assaulted. Where did things go so wrong for poor Mia? It couldn't have been her overzealous attempt to find meaning to her life by hoarding children, could it?

Mia Farrow went on to adopt five more children in hopes of fulfilling her lifelong dream of becoming a Crazy Kid Lady and eventually driving herself off a cliff in a rebellious fit of insanity. We're still waiting for the second half to unfold.

I don't care which way you slice it, anyone who has a maternal obsession to this degree, has got to be out of their mind.

* * *

As I mentioned before, my mother is an eternal lover. She searched endlessly for the one. For most of my life, I assumed having the displeasure of observing her search was a curse. Looking back, it was anything but a curse. My mother gave me a platform that rested on a sea of experience. I was fortunate enough to have the opportunity to learn from her mistakes before I was old enough to make my own. My mother's ability to nearly drown in the depths of her own passion and then breeze back to the surface completely unscathed is a power only a handful of people are lucky enough to possess.

As a female, your innermost desire is to obtain power and control of your emotions and reactions. However, rooted in the yearning for power lays an insatiable appetite for love. And when that appetite blows the crazy-fuse, some women simply replace it, while others allow the sparks to fly.

I have a predisposition for craziness. It's not only in my genetic makeup, but biologically it's inherent. It's in my blood. Just like every woman on this earth.

My mother's love life purveyed the idea that men are fashioned to leave and in turn, I was granted the right to dispose of them when I saw fit. I was taught to stand behind my intuition. From what I knew, you could love a man unconditionally but eventually they will turn. They either turn on you or against you, and they flee with parts of you. I learned that no man was going to be worth my overall sanity.

However, what you learn and what you are taught can sometimes be two very different things, because I was taught not to lose hope. I was taught that the heart wants what the heart wants. And I was shown that it's important to believe in that. It's better to know who and what you are and give yourself a chance to understand it than to deny it or make excuses for it.

So I learned it's okay to be a little nuts. It's okay to battle mind and matter. It's ok to express yourself in ways you see fit. It's okay to lash out at your bedroom walls and cry for days on end. And, really, it's okay to stalk a man and his new girlfriend to the point where you're nearly willing to end your life. More on that later.

Finding a medium is the only true struggle. That happy place where the mind and the heart can live peacefully with what they've learned from what they were taught. Some of us never get there. Knowing what you're looking for is half the battle. Once you figure that out, the path of recklessness that you've paved becomes obsolete.

Learning that I actually had no idea who my real father was at five years old was probably the first traumatizing experience I was faced with. This set a precedent that I really shouldn't trust anyone. In the very early stages of my formative years, I was taught that someone hadn't taken responsibility for one half of my DNA and that the person who had taken responsibility had lied to me about it.

While I never strayed from the love I had for my mother, I began to harbor doubt. From there forward, I learned how to be adaptive to situations I was too young to even comprehend fully.

The relationships my mother engaged in after Max were never anything I took seriously. They all felt like stopovers, aside from Will. My mother's marriage to him temporarily rehabilitated my trust issues. Once it all fell apart I had no choice but to reinforce the wall I'd previously built.

* * *

Mia Farrow's most noteworthy relationship was probably the one she's least known for, her relationship with Frank Sinatra. She was married to him for two years. Frank fucking Sinatra. The ultimate womanizer. This is who constructed Mia's ideals. I don't care how much you love the man's music, Frank Sinatra was a prick and you can't even hate him for it. He was a king and he chose to live like one. He took what he wanted when he wanted it and felt absolutely no remorse for anything he left behind. Frank Sinatra was an asshole. Yeah, I said it.

I'm willing to bet this marriage catapulted Mia Farrow into a world of delusion and insecurity. Dating America's playboy can't be all that settling. Frank Sinatra did things his way. When he was presented with an idea that her fame as an actress could overshadow his, he handed her divorce papers, proving it was his way or no way at all.

* * *

My mother's relationship with Max is a great example of how being with a man who controls you or wants to control you can be both mentally abusive and empowering. After Max, my mother never took shit from anyone. But simultaneously it also led her on a repetitive path. She became wound up in the idea that so long as she knew when to walk away, she would always rise above, always be able to move forward. Rather than take a step back to learn from the experience so she could stop the damaging cycle, she continued to perpetuate it. My mother is a strong woman, but it took the better half of her life to learn that walking away from an unhealthy situation is only half the battle. Navigating around the next one is the other half.

My mother is about a four on the crazy-scale. The unabashed queen of resilience, is and will always be crazy. Probably not for any specific reason other than she has the correct anatomy.

Max, Neil, Will, Ben, and Glen were all assholes. They all provoked my mother's illusion and in turn they wound up doing things that forced her to leave. But blaming them would be unfair. She should have been looking for someone she wouldn't eventually have to walk away from.

My mother made the same mistake over and over and over again, each time expecting a different result.

* * *

Mia Farrow was driven to insanity. She's delusional and Woody Allen remains her eternal asshole. He took her security and with it Soon Yi, who is a symbol of her last remaining hope. Someone she trusted took advantage of her situation and by that point she was all out of love for men. She gave up and settled for a different type of love, maternal love, because children don't tend to stray. And if one does, like Soon Yi, there can be 12 more to fill that void.

With great craziness comes great responsibility and a girl needs to understand that if she wants to take a stroll through Asshole Valley, she's going to wind up in Crazy Town.

Chapter 2:
The Jock

"Sometimes you get the best light from a burning bridge."

—Don Henley

High school was a strange and curious time. Popularity was something I fell into quite effortlessly. Maybe I'm a giant cunt for saying that. Maybe someone I went to high school with, someone who happened to be slightly less lucky, someone we'll name 'High School Holly', is going to read this and think I'm a giant cunt for saying that. I don't know. But for the same reason I'm not attending my ten-year reunion next month, I really don't care, because at the end of the day, high school was merely a flaccid blip on the radar in the grand scheme of my life.

I was popular but undecided whether I wanted to be. Okay, maybe that's inaccurate. I definitely didn't want to be unpopular. Nobody wants to be unpopular in high school. But I also never wanted to be someone that people looked up to and I certainly never wanted all the social commitments. There were so many other girls who really invested time and effort into their social rank in high school. Any kind of attention would have been better spent on someone who, at the very least, wanted to be there.

High school only came easy to me because one day, in grade five, a group of mean girls decided I was interesting enough to join their clique… and from there forward popularity just sort of clung to me like a mean case of herpes. That's not to say I didn't have my enemies, because I certainly did. The older girls hated me. Half of them made threats to drug me and then cut my hair off at parties. A few years back, the ringleader of that circus happened to be my waitress at a restaurant and she served me a shot of Jack with an apology. I took it, because in this monotonous life, you take anything that comes with a whiskey chaser. And honestly, between high school and adulthood, I've managed to acquire a ton of female enemies; one less foe was probably a step in the right direction.

With popularity came demand. And as far as the teenage male population at my school was concerned, I was in demand. Though, I didn't really date much. I realize how incredibly narcissistic this sounds but stay with me. Through the course of high school, I had two boyfriends and a plethora of crushes on older boys and rock stars, namely Mike Ness and Brad, a senior I once saw win a fist fight at the skate park while keeping his cigarette lit.

My first boyfriend was my age. He was captain of the junior basketball team and equally as popular. I don't know if that was the only reason we dated, but it probably was. Looking back, we had nothing in common. Mickey and I looked good together with our manageable acne and awkward baby fat, but we were equally egocentric and that was our common ground. At a whopping 5'6" and with a propensity for drug abuse, he had dreams of being in the NBA. You can imagine how that turned out.

I played basketball in high school, but unlike every other girl on the team, I never had any delusions about my future with the sport. I wanted to be a doctor. At least I thought I wanted to be a doctor. Until I realized how much I hated school, and authority, and hospitals, and sick people, most people in general actually. Let's just say, becoming a doctor wasn't in the cards.

I wish I remembered how Mickey and I started dating, but honestly, I don't. One day we were friends and the next day we were making out in my best friend's basement when her dad stepped out for his beer league baseball practice. Parental guidance is flimsy in a small town that's built on a foundation of addiction and teen pregnancy. But leaving four horny teenagers to their own devices in a dark rec room on a Friday night is probably the least effective way of lowering either statistic.

I was 13 and this was my first full-blown make-out. After the boys left, I felt an overwhelming collision of excitement and guilt. I was one of those teenagers with a moral conscience, and it has always haunted me. Every time I did something that was against the rules, I'd feel this tremendous guilt cast its shadow over me like I'd just banged a hooker in my child's bed. In fact, my conscience is probably the only thing that's kept me from becoming that hooker.

Things just sort of spiraled after that. Friday we were making out in Astrid's basement and come Monday we were awkwardly holding hands in the hallway while whispers circled around us. I would sit at my desk in math class, observing the over-sized clock above the door as it would slowly tick-tock the hour away. I'd watch the second-hand crawl around the numeric face and I could hear the minute-hand click every 60 seconds. I felt like I was in a John Hughes movie. Waiting that hour before I could pass Mickey in the hallway was a teenager's torture. But when the bell finally rang, it all happened in slow motion to some ridiculously cheesy soundtrack in my head. We would casually glance up just in time to cross paths and it was as if everyone else faded away and the noise of our friends chirping around us deafened to a silence. We'd smile cockily at each other with perfectly scripted nonchalance and in a moment it was over and all the noise wound back up to speed. But that two-second smile got me through the next hour of PE or Science or whatever bullshit class I had ahead of me. I secretly started to plan my class-to-class routes around Mickey's, making sure I almost always walked past him, no matter how far out of the way it was.

Crazy Level: 3.2 A relatively comfortable level of crazy to maintain. A 3.2 is marriage material! Though, a 13-year-old is not.

We only had one class together, Social Studies. We sat across from each other, as couples generally would. He spent the entire semester copying my work. You'd think this probably should have been a sign, but I didn't mind knowing I was smarter than he was. I was so infatuated with him that I didn't really care if he preferred to jerk off than study. When he wasn't copying my work, Mickey was usually cracking jokes. Our teacher was a massive stoner so the jokes were usually at his expense. Mickey was so cool. You can't see my eyes roll, but they're rolling.

I guess I started to derail. My mother called it puppy love. I resented that term. How could she diminish my make-out obsession to something as pubescent as Puppy Love? This was the real deal. I was in love. Mickey and I were meant for each other. We were going to get married and I would take his last name because I'd already wasted hours upon hours practicing my new signature in basically every notebook I owned. Destiny was clearly knocking.

High school was basically just a smorgasbord of embarrassing choices, bad style and sexual anxiety, nervously plugging things into holes because you read about it in a *Cosmo* magazine. Growing up really gives you an opportunity to realize how disposable your youth was. Well, I guess some of us look back and realize how disposable it all was, others get knocked up at prom and spend nine years posting about how awesome being a young parent is on their Facebook page. They're the people who live for the opportunity to plan the high school reunion that no one interesting will attend. Anyone with a life is too busy enjoying that life to spend time and money catching up with a bunch of people they have nothing in common with anymore. If High School Holly didn't already think I was a cunt, she sure does now.

Let me quickly break it down here. There is a reason most people move on after graduation. It takes ten minutes after high school ends to realize that it was a pile of meaningless garbage. You keep in touch with the handful of people you've managed to relate to over the years and everyone else dissolves into the world of social media posts you happen upon at 3 AM when you can't sleep. Facebook has made high school reunions obsolete. You accept everyone who adds you because it's easier than explaining to them why you declined them when they privately message you. And it's an indirect way to stay in touch with people you wouldn't otherwise stay in touch with. Thanks to social media, I know when Brenda's child eats, sleeps, shits, walks, talks, and falls. I don't need to go to my high school reunion to hear all the stories

I already try to avoid on Facebook. And it's not because I think I'm better than anyone, I'm certainly not, it's because I just can't manage to give a flying shit no matter how hard I try. And small talk gives me anxiety. I don't want kids, I don't want to engage in uninformative chatter about your kids, and I don't want to reminisce the days when we were kids. Fuck kids. Not literally, because that's messed up.

That is why I'm choosing not to go to my high school reunion. I'd rather get drunk by myself in some shithole while I try to finish this book than give my social anxiety another chance to ruin a perfectly good afternoon.

My editor was best quoted, "You think I party too much? Yeah, well I think you have too many kids." I stand by this.

Anyways, back to my puppy love derailment. I wasn't expecting this kinder-obsession to turn the world upside down. But it did. I fell head over flat-soled heels. My days started to revolve around Mickey and my nights revolved around hearing from Mickey. Eventually the games ensued. If he didn't call me at night, I assumed something was wrong and wouldn't sleep through the night. The next day at school I would act blasé, even if he ignored me. I did my best to keep my cool because everyone was watching, but I was secretly going mad. Finally, at the end of the day, after ignoring me to spend lunch with his friends, he'd show up at my locker asking to walk home together. Sometimes I'd oblige, other times I would lie and say I had plans with my friends. I had no idea what I was doing, but my inconsistency drove him mad too. I didn't realize he was testing me, testing my limits and what he could get away with. I just assumed he was being a little prick and I knew my best bet was to give him a taste of his own medicine. But his games ensued.

We wound up breaking up and getting back together many times throughout that school year (I almost want to put quotations around breaking up and getting back together because that's how hilariously meaningless it all was).

Mickey had my locker combination. So every time he did something insensitive or blatantly idiotic, he would leave an apology letter in my locker that I would find between my classes.

We made an attempt to always attend each other's basketball games, even if we were fighting. In fact, I would show up especially if we were fighting, looking my absolute best with an army of my hot girlfriends. We'd be loud and obnoxious in the most flirtatious way we knew how and all the older boys would crowd around us. This ignited exactly the reaction I'd hoped for. It made Mickey angry but it kept him interested. And more importantly, it kept me in first place.

When the basketball game ended, he would race out of the change room to the foyer and there I would be, casually chatting with my friends. He would beeline for my cheek to plant a dramatic kiss, ultimately pissing on his territory. And in those fleeting moments, I knew I'd won. Every teenage boy has Attention Deficit Disorder when it comes to girls. It's science. You've got to use your immaturity to your advantage so they keep pining over you, otherwise they'll find someone else to pine over.

Come the end of my first year of high school, I was pretty sure I had the whole dating thing figured out. I had my boyfriend on a prover-bial leash and I was able to tighten and release the slack whenever I wanted. I had only allowed him to go to first base. Make-outs and the occasional feel-up, which felt more like mammograms than a grasp at sexual curiosity, were all I was offering. But my adorable attempt to preserve my innocence was eventually outvoted by my complete lack of personal standard.

* * *

Summer kicked off with a bang.

I grew up with a big backyard and it was tradition to host sleepovers with my girlfriends on the trampoline in the summer. Waking up with dew clammed to your face and bugs crawling all over you were things worth living for, I guess.

One night, Astrid came over and we packed all the blankets and pillows onto the trampoline. She was dating Mickey's friend, Eric, at the time so once my folks were asleep, we called the boys. They snuck out and rode their bikes across town before hopping the fence into my backyard. We decided to engage in a cultured game of Truth or Dare. When it was Astrid's turn, Eric dared her to run around the yard topless. So, she did. The game basically ended there because once there's nudity, there isn't really anywhere to go from there but down. We broke out into two separate make-out frenzies, rolling around the trampoline. Mickey and I wound up on one side of the trampoline while Astrid and Eric dry-humped on the other side. We were flipping around under the blankets like two puppies with fleas when Mickey's hand reached into my underwear.

Let me reiterate, summer kicked off with a bang. Sorry, Dad.

We spent the rest of the summer fooling around. We mastered the art of digital sex, which these days has an entirely different meaning. I wasn't willing to go any further so Mickey settled for whatever he could get.

* * *

A new girl moved to town late that summer. Karen was a long-legged blonde and her parents were easygoing pot-smokers who allowed her to throw parties every weekend. Unfortunately, I wasn't really allowed to go to any of them unless her parents were going to chaperone. Most of the time I just lied and said her parents were there. Other times, they were actually there.

This was when having two cops for parents became problematic. One night, I had to sneak out to go to one of Karen's parties because my parents caught wind that her folks were out of town. Around 10 PM, we received a noise complaint, and to my misfortune my dad happened to be on duty that night. When I heard someone yell, "COPS!" I ran downstairs, frantically searching for somewhere to hide. I found a closet and ducked inside, closing the sliding door behind me.

I could hear my dad walking through the house, asking the kids questions, ultimately searching for beer, weed and his problematic daughter. I heard him come into the room I was hiding in and circle around. He asked Karen if she'd seen me that night. Karen lied. My dad slapped her with a casual warning and told her to turn the music down because the neighbors were complaining. I think I held my breath the entire time it took my dad to circle that room. I was petrified. When I heard him leave I burst out of the closet, gasping dramatically like the archetypal virgin in a slasher flick.

I sighed with relief, but relief quickly turned to panic when I realized that he was probably heading home to check in on me. I had to get there first. I tried to find Mickey before I left to tell him I was leaving but he was nowhere in sight. I had no choice but to get the fuck out of there if I wanted to spare myself another grounding.

I hitched a ride from one of the older kids and snuck in through my bedroom window. I didn't know if someone was going to be home, so the window was a safe choice. Four minutes later, my dad came through the front door. I could hear the sound his work boots made as he stomped down the hallway toward my room. He knocked on my bedroom door before entering and found me, sitting in my pajamas on my bed, watching *Silence of the Lambs*.

"Just popped in to say hi!" he said cheerfully.

"Uh huh," I responded with all my teenage angst.

"Okay then. I should get back to work, I guess..." he veered off and started to close my door. But just before it closed shut, he swung it open again. "I know we told you that you couldn't go to that party tonight because it wasn't chaperoned. I'm sorry if you feel like you're missing out. You're a good kid."

I smiled back, "Dad, this is the part where Lecter wears the cop's face to escape, you're killing me here."

He laughed, "Night kiddo."

"Night," I replied.

Irony.

I heard all kinds of rumors about Mickey the following day. I heard he was caught kissing Karen and stayed over at her house. I heard he had kissed multiple girls. I heard he and Karen slept in the same bed. I heard a million different stories, each one contradicting the last. It was a small town. People didn't really have a lot to do.

When I didn't hear from Mickey for three days, I decided waiting around for him to acknowledge me was useless. I went out with my friends. I went out with his friends. I just went out. Everyone told me he wanted to break up with me, that he liked Karen now and that he was too afraid to tell me himself. I was heart-broken but I pretended not to care.

Finally, he called me. I didn't answer. The phone rang eight times and I refused to answer it. Call display had just come on the scene and it changed the game. He called again. I didn't answer. He called a third time. I didn't answer so he left a message. I never called him back.

I decided to spend the last week of my summer enjoying myself, so I surrounded myself with friends and activities to keep my mind away from his phone calls. He had continued to call that entire week. Finally, the weekend before school started, I answered.

"What? If you're calling to break up with me, you're an idiot, because as far as I'm concerned, I've been single for the last two weeks," I said.

"I'm not calling to break up with you," he slowly replied.

"Then what?" I asked.

"I'm calling because I'm sorry. I shouldn't have acted that way. It was immature. I didn't make out with Karen or anyone. I crashed at her place, but I spent the night smoking weed with her brother. I just thought maybe I didn't want a girlfriend anymore. But I do."

Long, dramatic pause. "So, what then? You're calling because you want to get back together or something?"

"Yes."

Long, dramatic pause. "Okay, cool," I responded.

"Well, what are you doing?" He asked.

"About to watch a movie."

"Are your parents working?"

"Yes… do you want to come over?"

"I'll be there in ten minutes!" he exclaimed.

In 11 minutes, we were on the couch with our hands down each other's pants.

* * *

Grade nine was off to a rocky start. Astrid's parents had gotten a divorce and her mom met someone new. She moved the whole family to Nanaimo, a city 20 miles away from Ladysmith. Which meant Astrid was going to a new school. This was devastating for a 14-year-old. Being popular didn't matter. When the one person you can count on moves away, you suddenly feel very alone. Everyone secretly loves to hate you when they feel threatened by you, and I'd become vulnerable without my best friend.

Preparing for utter devastation, I went into the ninth grade with a wall up and a chip on my shoulder. That might sound dramatic, mostly because it was.

At least I had Mickey. We spent most of our time fawning and falling all over each other like a couple of idiots. Everything seemed to be working out between us. The summer was just a minor hiccup. Mickey learned his lesson and now we could finish high school, and get married, and live happily ever after. He would never make another mistake like that again. Because you know, 14-year-olds are so deeply conscious-minded and care so much about how their actions affect other people.

* * *

About two weeks into my second year of high school, a new girl came to town. Blonde, petite and completely dense, Claire was every small-town boy's wet dream. We were all jealous. Her perfect skin and her big, confused blue eyes had nothing on her giant water balloon boobs. They looked like they were enslaved, begging to be freed from the oppression of her electric pink bra under her tight, white t-shirt. She reeked of endorphins and wore a distinct perfume, Eau De Fuck-Me-in-the-Darkroom. Every guy in school wanted a run at Claire. Not to anyone's surprise, every guy also got one, but Mickey was the first.

The day I saw her walk through the foyer doors, I felt a ripple under my feet. I looked around, curious if anyone else felt the beginnings of an earthquake. And when no one stirred, I knew it was just the crumbling of my entire romantic future. I looked over at Mickey while he ogled the new girl. As Claire's boobs slowly bounced past our table, her gaze met Mickey's and she flashed him a flirtatious smile. My glare swapped from him to her, back to him. And then rested on her. I sized her up and down because I knew I was in for a fight. I knew I had met my arch nemesis.

Who did I think I was? Luke Skywalker?

It wasn't long before my relationship with Mickey started to fizzle. I would catch him flirting with Claire in the hallway between classes and when she saw me coming, she would cower and scramble away. While she may have had the upper hand with Mickey, she knew that I could destroy her social life. With popularity comes great power and greater pettiness.

One day after the final bell rang and school let out, Mickey showed up at my locker and asked to walk me home. Which was pretty normal, until we left the grounds and he suddenly had nothing to say. His silence was unbearable.

"So, what's up?" I asked.

"Oh nothing…" he trailed off.

"Well, something is definitely wrong. What is it?"

"I, I don't know. Nothing is wrong, I just. I don't think this is really working out anymore."

"So, you asked to walk me home to break up with me?" I asked.

Long, dramatic pause. "I think so," he finally replied.

My eyes started to well up. I could feel myself about to lose control and stopped. I took a deep breath, "Is this because you like Claire?"

"No," he started. "Well, maybe. I mean we are so much alike, and she just gets me. You know?"

Does She get you? Fuck you, you little asshole. Fuck you and fuck her and fuck your bullshit excuses. What does that even mean? You dubious fuck. I hope you walk away from this conversation and get hit by a bus. Douche. Fuck you.

I mean, that's what I wanted to say. Instead, I just glared at him, with the most condescending resting bitch face I could pull off. "Good for you," I uttered. And then I walked away.

Asshole Rating: 3.9 I've cut Mickey slack here because of his age. High school is confusing and weird, and puberty gets in the way of your conscience. It's unfair to give someone an honest asshole rating when their balls haven't even dropped yet.

When I stepped through my front door, I closed it behind me and involuntarily began to bawl. I fell back against the door and somberly slid down until I reached the floor, cupping my cheekbones to catch my tears. I cried and cried. Thankfully no one was home, so I didn't have to explain this hideous, melodramatic meltdown.

I pretended that I was sick for the rest of the week.

Mickey finally called Saturday afternoon. I didn't answer because, fuck him.

He called again that night. I still didn't answer. He called right through until Sunday night. I remained strong.

On Monday morning, I finally got out of bed and looked at my reflection in the mirror. The past five days had really taken a toll on me. I looked like I'd risen from the dead. I let out a sigh and decided to hop in the shower. I couldn't hide in bed forever. Well maybe I could, but bedsores are gross. I had to face the fire.

I slowly got ready for school, careful to do my makeup just right. If I was ready to make a comeback, I had to look fresh and unfazed. Actually, I had to look better than I've ever looked before. I'd lost about five pounds in five days. Depression is the always the best diet, next to cocaine of course. I slipped on the tightest pair of jeans I owned and looked at my reflection in the mirror. They fit better than ever. Satisfied with my dehydrated frame, I scoured my closet for the sexiest top I owned and slid it on over my push-up bra. I took one final look in the mirror. Revenge is bittersweet, a lesson that only becomes more relevant the older you get.

I took a deep breath before I yanked on the front door to the school foyer. I slipped into the crowded area just as the bell rang to indicate a five-minute warning to get to class. A large group of my friends were sitting around a table and one by one, they all turned to look at me. No one moved, despite the bell's urgency. I looked over to my audience and smirked. I could see Mickey in my peripheral. I didn't bat an eye. Instead, I turned down the hallway toward my locker in the opposite direction.

My friends chased after me. Once they caught up, they all chimed in at once, like crows flocking to a dead carcass. They immediately began spouting off rumors about Mickey and Claire, begging to know what really happened between us. I shrugged it off, refusing to divulge the truth. It was no one's business and the more they pried, the more I realized that none of these people really cared about my wellbeing. They just wanted to create noise.

After the gossip convention dispersed, I gathered my math books from my locker. Just as I was about to shut the door, I felt a tap on my shoulder. I looked over as Mickey casually leaned against the locker next to mine. I looked at him and my smile faded.

"You seem to be doing okay, considering everything," he stated. Facetious bastard.

My stare remained indifferent as I coldly responded, "I guess you could say that some things aren't worth the bother. How's Claire?"

"She's fine..." he trailed off. "I miss you though."

"I can't imagine what that must feel like." I laughed as I slammed my locker door shut. I watched him condescendingly as I shoved the brand-new lock into place. He looked at the lock suspiciously. I turned on my heel with a smile before I marched down the hallway, away from my Disney movie.

It was probably for the best. A teacher had picked up on Mickey's plagiarism and I wasn't about to sink with that ship. Best he learned what failure felt like before his drug addiction surfaced and his growth spurt didn't.

CHAPTER 2.5:
INDIFFERENCE

*"You know the main thing in life? A sense of humor. Lose that,
you're done. You might as well blow your fucking brains out."*

—Lemmy Kilmister

THEY say that your first heartbreak is always the worst. That's probably untrue. You can't really trust what "they" say, because "they"
are usually a group of young men sitting around a woodstove in the
dark with horseshit stuck to the bottom their shoes, discussing the
benefits of slavery while an oppressed housewife who's never voted
or touched money serves them dinosaur skewers and butter-less bread
rolls. Maybe this adage was true 200 years ago when people only lived
to be 30 and their first heartbreak happened at the age of 15, because
their husband of three years contracted syphilis and then actually died
from it.

So, while maybe your first heartbreak isn't necessarily going to be
your worst, it will probably be the most ridiculous. Learning the ef-
fect of loss in your young adolescence is an absolute nightmare. You're
hardly a human being yet. The only life skills you've learned at that
point are the ones your parents have taught you—and whatever epipha-
nies you've taken from The Simpsons. You feel incredibly alone because
most of the people you know haven't dealt with heartbreak yet. At 14,
most kids are too busy jerking off to their dad's porn magazines or making out with Marky Mark's Calvin Klein ad. I guess that's probably

an irrelevant reference nowadays. If your teenage daughter is caught making out with photos of a half-naked Mark Wahlberg, you've got a bigger issue on your hands.

The excitement that comes attached to your first love is something you can't compare to anything else. My experience with the Jock left me on a wild goose chase for a specific type of asshole, one that I would continue to hunt for well into my twenties. To write an entire book that essentially encompasses relationship failure, this obviously didn't work out in my favor. I became engrossed in the chase. Attaining the unattainable– the ongoing, and impeccably delirious quest to tame the damaged boy.

What you don't realize when you're young and lacking any kind of relationship experience is that the unattainable is unattainable and damaged because they've chosen to be. And trying to fix what technically isn't broken is only going to drive you to the madhouse. Insanity is, sadly, a fish you can catch. Metaphorically of course, for any idiots out there.

* * *

Let's take a plaid-smeared stroll through the ´90s for a minute to dissect grunge music's perfect cum-shot, the late Kurt Cobain. This was a guy who was so riddled with angst, that he actually blew a hole through his own face. Allegedly. Though, I imagine that being married to Courtney Love would drive any man eight feet deep, one way or another.

Of course, there are theories that Courtney killed her husband, and really, I guess it's plausible. There's no question that she's off her nut and mentally unstable enough to hire a hit man. She's certifiably crazy. We all saw her at the roast of Pam Anderson. She looked like she got caught in Hurricane Katrina on her way to the studio. Drugs will turn you insane and it's no secret that Courtney Love has come in Betty Ford's back door more times than the ex-president. Potentially untrue, but completely hilarious.

Is she crazy enough to kill someone? Who knows? Probably? Her father sure thinks so. And so do thousands of manic Nirvana fans. Do I? Nah.

But let's be honest here, Kurt Cobain was no patron saint of apathy. He was a giant, gaping asshole. The question here is who led whom to their breaking point? Was Courtney so crazy that she pushed Kurt to end his life or was Kurt such a prick that he led her to utter madness?

Her father has claimed that they were on the outs prior to Kurt's death. They were headed for divorce and he'd made multiple threats to change his will. Maybe Courtney took an opportunity. Maybe Kurt had a bizarre affinity for ironic timing. Maybe he wanted the public to blame Courtney in the heat of a conflict. Maybe he was bipolar. Maybe he was doing a blanket favor to everyone involved by ending his misery. The reasons people have for committing suicide aren't really up for debate in. If a person chooses to take their dirt nap early, well, it's their choice to make.

Leaving your daughter to grow up under the supervision of an addict is kind of a dick move, though. At least give the poor kid a chance. It can't be easy learning your life lessons from someone who's been chasing the dragon for so long she's probably forgotten chasing the dragon is just a trope. If Kurt's death was the product of suicide, which it probably was, he's more of an asshole than Courtney would be crazy if she had killed him.

With all sincerity, I can imagine being in a position where you think for a minute that maybe, just maybe, it would be easier to live without someone you love on this earth than it would be to live with their existence and without their love. Maybe. If after re-reading that last statement you find yourself thinking, "this person is a fucking lunatic, I could never imagine killing anyone," you're probably much crazier than I am. We've all imagined killing someone, so don't pretend you're above murder. Not only have you thought of homicide, but you're also in complete denial of it and capable of believing your own lies. Which is messed up. You need a therapist, Dahmer.

* * *

It's safe to say that my relationship with The Jock ended more maturely than any other relationship since. You're so fresh and full of your own charm when you're a kid that when you get an idea in your head, you run with it. You don't let your feelings get in the way of your actions because you know you can't afford the wayward humiliation. At the end of every long and arduous day, it is imperative that you save face. You have to be cool, and nothing is cooler than indifference. So, you react to a situation, shake it off and roll on. In high school, all that matters is who winds up on top. If you want to remain desirable, you can't go crawling back to your mistakes. You wake up five pounds skinnier, put on your hottest outfit, force a mysterious smile over your teeth, and pretend like you've been bedridden with strep throat for the past week. There is no time for obsession. You forfeit being crazy to be the bigger asshole.

If only we knew now what we once knew then.

Sadly, this is a lesson that no woman carries into adulthood. Imagine how dominant the female population could be if we'd stuck to our high school morals: #1. Always break up on top and #2. Know your butthole's worth. Seriously ladies, save anal for marriage, life isn't a rodeo.

In fact, I'm going to touch on that for a minute. There's a reason marriage has become so lackluster in the past 50 years. It's because there's nothing really sacred about it anymore. There's nothing special, no surprises. It's often used as an attempt to remedy the fact that you don't even really like each other. You've got to hang onto something for marriage and let's face it no one is waiting for their wedding day to have sex anymore unless there's something wrong with them. And maybe that thing is religion, but maybe it's also 12-inch labia.

So listen, if anal is out of the question because you accidently gave that up on prom night to some loser named Justin who wore skate shoes with his suit, consider saving something else sacred for marriage, like your grandmother's peach cobbler recipe... or bukkake.

* * *

Maybe Kurt would still be alive if Courtney just walked away when the divorce papers were served. Maybe Francis Bean (seriously, who named this child?) would have a better chance at something beyond a sequel to her parents' tragedy if Courtney just walked away. Maybe she still does. Maybe she's found a way to adapt in order to rise above the madness. Maybe she learned from her parents' mistakes. Or maybe she watches a lot of Simpsons.

Let's not get this twisted, I'm not choosing sides on a debate that is over two decades old. What I'm saying here is this: if money can buy Magic Johnson the cure for HIV, it's not a stretch that maybe money could also buy Courtney Love's innocence.

* * *

I never dreamed of killing the Jock. Not even when I was hiding in bed for a week. I felt like my heartbreak was a phase, something I could get over if I put my mind to it. Just like the inspirational poster in *Teen Beat* said, because that's what survival consists of when you're 14: bad reading material and inspirational bullshit.

I was young and resilient. I started to act a little obsessive but caught it just in time to reel it in before it was too late. I saw the edge from afar and I backed away from it, assuming dark consequences were ahead. I was neither willing nor ready to exercise that demon yet. Unfortunately, at 14 I was wiser than I would grow up to be.

That round everyone got out alive and I wound up on top. Sadly, the opposite was true for Kurt Cobain. I guess he lost his sense of humor.

Maybe Kurt was murdered, maybe he wasn't. Does anyone honestly give a flying toss anymore? At the end of the day, if Courtney didn't kill the gatekeeper of grunge, it's likely that he would have offed himself anyways. You can't suffer the wrath of a woman with more issues than National Geographic longer than the dating period. Kurt fucked up; he married certifiably crazy. Every man knows you never marry a woman who is certifiably crazy.

Because certifiably crazy might just open up a can of suicide on your ass.

CHAPTER 3:
THE CHEATER

"The Edge... There is no honest way to explain it because the only people who really know where it is are the ones who have gone over. The others—the living—are those who pushed their control as far as they felt they could handle it, and then pulled back, or slowed down, or did whatever they had to when it came time to choose between Now and Later. But the edge is still out there."

—Dr. Hunter S. Thompson

I F I can impart one very important piece of advice to anyone who has yet to fall down the lunacy vortex, it's this: Don't. Look that evil, dark beast square in the eye, raise your middle finger, casually turn around and sprint wildly in the opposite direction. There is no time for contemplation. There is no time for curiosity. Get the hell out of there, because nothing that lies ahead will be able to save you from yourself.

Unfortunately, no one gave me this advice. Or any constructive, helpful advice at all. "Follow your heart, Jordan," that's what they all said. If anyone ever tells you to follow your heart, punch that idiot in the face. It's a trap. You know what your heart leads you to? Self-destruction, that's what. "Follow your heart," is a phrase that was probably originally smeared on a bathroom wall in the blood of a crazed junkie who was desperately searching for a vein to stab.

Follow your gut and nothing else. Ever. If your gut tells you something isn't right, something probably isn't right, and you are in no position to argue. Pack your bags and check out. Don't take chances, because chances lead to momentum and momentum leads to tripping and tripping leads to falling right over that motherfucking cliff. I promise.

* * *

I met Billy on a hot, summer afternoon while catching a little sun by the river with my friend, Jill. At the time, we were about 16 and Jill was dating a senior. Adam, a pseudo redneck turned sex-addict was Jill's first and the only thing either of them could talk about after doing the deed, was the deed. I felt like I'd lost my own virginity listening to the stories that provoked her self-appointed accolade of sexual hierarchy.

I knew that Adam planned to meet us that afternoon but when I saw him emerge from the forested path with Billy, I couldn't hide my pathetic schoolgirl excitement. Jill noticed the wad of drool drip from the corner of my mouth and nudged me back to reality, "Pull it together, will you?"

I looked at her and wiped my jaw.

I'd always known who Billy was. He was six years older than I was but it didn't matter. I'd been in love with him since the first time I saw him on that fall afternoon when he drove past me in his midnight blue Monte Carlo. He was a green-eyed God. Every young girl in Ladysmith had a crush on Billy Davidson, even Jill.

Billy smiled at me as they approached our set-up on the massive boulder. Jill began to greet him, but he cut her off and extended his hand in my direction to introduce himself. Billy was dating Adam's older sister at the time and everyone in town knew it. He was intimidating because he was off-limits, and he knew it.

I decided I needed to cool down and wash away whatever pathetic fangirl sweat I'd accumulated, so I grabbed Jill and together we jumped into the river. Billy didn't waste a second. He lifted his shirt over his head, stepped out of his shoes and dove in after us. Adam stood on the rocks and reached into the cooler. He pulled out four beers and tossed them one by one down to Billy as he treaded water. Billy handed us a beer as Adam undressed and dove off the small cliff.

Despite having a girlfriend, Billy spent the afternoon flirting like a bachelor. And I shamelessly flirted back. After a few hours splashing around in the river, Jill and I climbed back onto the rock to dry off in the sun as Billy and Adam sat on the bank in the shade on the other side of the river. Adam appeared to be in deep conversation, cursing aggressively while his hands waved back and forth, but Billy wasn't paying much attention to him. He just sat there, across the river, staring directly at me. The guy was guiltless. Normally, you would consider this the behavior of a predator, but predators aren't that attractive. It's just science.

I snapped out of his gaze when Adam eventually clued into our staring contest. I diverted all of my attention back to Jill's superfluous tales of sexual experimentation.

* * *

The following weeks passed as summer began to wind down to a close. At the time, I was working at McDonald's.

One evening, around 6 PM, I left work after a long dayshift. I was wearing the hideous green uniform, complete with a visor, nametag, grease stains and self-pity. As I drove past the ball field, a motorcycle sped past me in the opposite direction. I glanced into my rearview mirror and shook my head at the driver's obvious disregard for the speed limit. I noticed the faint blinking of the motorcycle's brake lights in the distance. I found that odd as the next stop sign wasn't for another quarter mile or so, but he disappeared as I turned a corner. I made a few more turns before the long stretch of road that led to my block.

I was almost home when I heard a sharp buzz from behind me. I looked into my rearview mirror and froze in horror. The same motorcycle was quickly gaining on me. What the hell was wrong with this guy? I sped up to race home. When I pulled into my driveway, I saw the motorcycle come blazing around the corner. I got out of my car and he slowed down, stopping next to the curb about 15 feet in front of me. I glared at the faceless stranger, on the verge of utter rage as he removed his helmet.

I quickly realized that the creep wasn't a deranged madman. The creep was Billy. He sized me up and down in my frumpy, grease-stained uniform. I quickly removed the stupid visor from my head and nervously fumbled around. I was trapped in a bad Wes Anderson movie. A department store of emotions flooded over me as he turned off the engine. I was conflicted between excitement, irritation and embarrassment.

"Does your girlfriend know you follow girls home from work?" I quipped.

"I can't imagine her caring. We broke up last week," he replied as he coolly ran his fingers through his hair to brush the flyaway strands off his forehead.

"I see," I replied, forcing back a smile.

Billy made small talk, he was nervous and I went out of my way to make him feel uncomfortable. I didn't trust him and I certainly didn't trust myself around him. After beating endlessly at the wall I'd put up, he finally gave up with a huff. He started his bike and before he lifted his helmet over his perfect head, he flashed a curious smile, "So I guess I'll see you around then?"

"Maybe," I pathetically replied in a failed attempt to sound cooler than him. I might as well have farted.

He smoothly pulled the masked helmet over his head and snapped the chinstrap into place, returning to the faceless stranger.

* * *

The next month was daunting. Billy figured out my email address and added me on MSN Messenger. If you don't remember what that was, you have no business reading this book.

We exchanged messages here and there. I was careful to keep it brief. I didn't know what I wanted from him. If I even wanted anything at all. I knew my schoolgirl crush was toxic and my only bet was to tread very lightly.

Looking back, keeping our exchanges so brief all the time probably roused Billy. He definitely wasn't the type of guy who was familiar with rejection. And honestly, the only reason I was the way I was with him, was my lack of experience. I was reacting honestly because I had no clue how to fake it. Which is ironic because faking it eventually becomes the one skill all women are familiar with.

One Saturday night I was at home, playing around on the computer when a chat box notification appeared. I had forgotten that I was even online. I clicked on the notification. It was Billy. *"What you up to?"*

I stared at the typed message for a few minutes, unsure whether I wanted to respond or not. But curiosity (and obsession) got the best of me, as it always does when you're a teenager. *"Not much... Saturday night and you have nowhere better to be?"* I responded.

I waited while he typed. *"Everyone is at the Timberland, didn't feel like going... I was going to grab a case of beer and head to the boat docks, maybe listen to some music."* There was a short pause before he continued to type. I waited anxiously, staring at the computer screen before his message appeared, *"Interested?"*

And there it was. I paused, frozen in this stupid eclipse of time. I felt like I was Molly Ringwald at the end of, well, every film she's ever starred in. My heart began to race over the cool, older guy. Every ounce of my body broke into shivers and hives. I was so nervous that my fingers took over as I typed: *"Sorry, curfew is eleven thirty. It's already nine."*

There was a long pause before he dropped offline. My heart sank. I'd made a mistake. Regret clung to me like a giant leech. I was about to logout so I could sulk in my bedroom. But then, like a sudden aftershock of unbridled ecstasy, he appeared again. And like a drug coursing through my veins, unwilling to compromise his intention, he said, *"I'm going to be there in twenty minutes. Get ready. You'll be home by curfew."* And he signed off, this time leaving no room for a response. I stared at the computer screen in disbelief. I was going on a date with Billy Davidson.

Both of my parents were working that night so I called my dad to tell him that I was going to a movie with Jill and I would be home at curfew. He didn't ask any questions so I raced to my bedroom in a typical teenage panic over what to wear. I dug through my drawers searching for the sexiest bra I owned. I quickly threw it on before changing into a fresh t-shirt and jeans.

He showed up five minutes early. Luckily, I was ready when I heard him honk from the driveway. For those of you who don't remember MSN messenger and have continued to read, this is how we did things before text messaging existed. As I made my way down my driveway, he got out of the truck and shuffled around to the passenger side. He opened the door and extended a hand to help me into the truck. Like a goddamned gentleman. This is probably still the most chivalrous thing that's ever happened to me. Aside from the time I was in New Orleans and a male stripper offered me a handkerchief after he sat me on a stage, tilted my head back and dragged his balls across my face.

Billy hopped back into the driver's seat and looked at me with excitement, "Ready?" he asked.

"Born ready," I replied. Which would later prove to be a very definitive moment in our relationship, because I wasn't ready. Not even a little bit.

We made our way down to the boat docks. There's an eerie part of the drive through the forest that, even in the safest of circumstances, you contemplate the possibility of being stopped by some deranged hermit disguised as a civilian in distress before you're dragged to his secluded cabin, where he would sedate you and then surgically attach your mouth to a stranger's anus.

So I had a moment.

Billy parked close to the shore and turned the key back in the ignition. The music continued to play. He reached forward and swung his arm toward me. I jumped out of my seat, expressing every ounce of teenage nervousness. He laughed as he continued to reach into the back seat and grabbed two bottles of beer.

"Thirsty?" he patronized.

I looked at him with frustration and grabbed one of the bottles from his hand.

He laughed. "Why are you always so cold? You need to lighten up."

I glared at him. No one had ever called me cold before, surprisingly. I didn't know how to respond. I took a sip of beer and stared out at the ocean through the windshield, "Maybe you're just too warm."

He stared at me like I'd just recited sixty digits of Pi. "You're interesting," he said. Billy wasn't a genius, but luckily for him, he sure was pretty.

I probably blushed. I wanted to be the type of girl Billy Davidson might be interested in, but it was in my vulnerability that he was most enamored; the bitterness I'd always assumed was uncool and tried to suppress.

Jack and Diane beamed over the speaker. Billy asked me if I knew who sang the song.

I laughed at him. "Yeah, I think so."

He reached over and started to trace shapes on my leg. "You're having a hard time remembering because you're nervous," he flashed an evil, seductive smile.

"I know who it is," I said as I scrambled for the name of an artist I was embarrassingly familiar with.

He looked at me and said, "I'll give you a hint." He started to trace the letters 'J' and 'O' on my knee while he stared at me devilishly and taunted, "Still not sure?"

I innocently shook my head as he traced the letter 'H' over my thigh.

The answer suddenly came to me but I kept my mouth shut, allowing him to trace John Cougar Mellencamp's excruciatingly long name on my upper thigh. The sexual tension escalated as he grazed the intersecting cross-seam of my jeans. He reached up and gently slid his hand behind my head, staring at me intently while John's lyrics about being 16 that expand over the 2:46 and 2:54 minute mark blared at me through the speaker. (Note: quoting song lyrics in a book is a massive pain in the ass. So to avoid doing more work than I already have to, I'll wait while you Google it.)

Got it? Great.

I wish I were joking about the timing of this song; that this was a strategic move to sell this story. Unfortunately, it's not. My life has basically just been a continuous stream of embarrassing, ironic memes.

If you can't imagine where this cliché is going, he kissed me. And I kissed him back, harder than I'd ever kissed any pillow in my pathetic life. I climbed over the console to straddle him. We moved up and down with the kiss before he lifted my shirt over my head, exposing my generic white bra. At 16 years old, the sexiest bra you own is usually just the one with the fewest sweat stains and a back clasp. As his curious hands made their way to the button of my jeans, an unfamiliar ringtone blasted over the music. I pulled back as the ringing continued. He sighed, reaching into his pocket and pulling out a silver cellphone.

He looked at the front display with confusion, "It's my brother's friend, I feel like I should take this." He flipped the phone open and casually brought it to his ear, "Hey? Jason?" He listened for a while and then broke into laughter. "Yeah, give me twenty minutes, I'll be there," he said. He shifted the speaker away from his mouth as he whispered to me, "You aren't going to believe this."

I leapt off him, back over the console, into the passenger seat and slid my shirt back over the sexiest bra I owned.

Billy closed the phone and turned the ignition, "Jason and a couple of his buddies went 4x4ing drunk. Now they're stuck in a river and need some help," he said as he took off back towards the eerie woods. "It's nearly past your curfew, I should probably get you home."

I laughed. "Or?"

He looked at me curiously. "I have to run home to grab some things. What if I drop you off first and give you a chance to settle in? Think you can sneak away for a couple hours? I promise this will be worth it."

I hesitated for a minute. I was terrified of my parents. If I were caught, I'd be in a world of shit. But adventure and infatuation got the best of me. "Sure, I think I can manage that."

Billy raced back to my house.

The phone rang as I walked through the front door. I knew it was my mother checking in to make sure I was home on time. I walked into the kitchen, picked up the receiver and answered, "Hello?"

"Oh good, you're home. How was your night?" she inquired.

I knew she wasn't really interested. "Nothing exciting. Jill and Adam fought over the ending the whole way home, but you know."

"Okay, honey. I just wanted to check in. Have a good night, love you," she relayed.

"You too. Don't get shot," I said sarcastically.

"Brat, you'd feel pretty terrible if that were to actually happen," she threw back.

I laughed. "Yeah, I guess you're right. Please don't get shot for real. Love you, good night."

"Night," she replied before hanging up.

I hung up the receiver and ran into my bedroom. I moved toward my bed and quickly tossed a stack of clean clothes and pillows under my blanket to create the illusion of a body sleeping. I propped my childhood teddy bear at the top of the silhouette in hopes that it would match my brown hair. I walked over to the switch on the wall and turned off the lights to evaluate the realness of my makeshift silhouette. The hallway light beamed in from the crack in the doorway as I peered in on my masterpiece. Satisfied, I smiled and closed my bedroom door. All that wasted time watching afterschool specials had finally paid off. I waited in the living room for Billy's truck to pull up.

Suddenly, I saw headlights beam through the front window. I sprang up from the couch and excitedly ran toward the window. It wasn't Billy. I started to panic.

I scrambled as I heard the key jiggle around in the lock before it finally clicked. The door flew open and my dad's voice boomed through the house, "Jordan, you home?"

I sprang around the corner.

"Oh, you are here. Just thought I'd pop by and check in."

"Well I'm here and mom already called," I fired at him.

He shot me a look of disapproval, "We worry you know."

"Canadian town of eight thousand people, it's practically Compton out there," I said sarcastically. "Big night cracking down on Lady-smith's pothead problem?"

"Yeah, yeah. What are you going to do now?" he asked, ignoring my tone.

"My super old boyfriend is going to come over and I guess we'll get high and then have unprotected sex in your bed."

"Can't even drop the sarcasm for a minute, huh?" he asked.

"Nope."

Suddenly, the dispatcher came over the radio attached to his belt. "Constable West, we have a domestic on the corner of third and Kitchener that needs your assistance."

My dad unclipped the radio from its holster. "Ten four," he said into the speaker. He reattached the radio to his belt. "See, it's not all potheads," he said to me.

I chuckled.

"Alright, I've got to run. Enjoy the rest of your night, kid."

"You too, Dad," I called as he rushed out the door. I watched him from the front window as he got into his cruiser and backed out of the driveway.

He drove past Billy's truck parked half a block down the street. Once my dad was out of sight, Billy's headlights flickered on and he drove up to the end of my driveway. I walked out the front door, locking it behind me and ran over to the passenger side of his truck.

"Close call," I said as I hopped inside.

We drove out to Cassidy where the boys were stranded. When we arrived, we spotted Kyle standing in creek next to the truck wearing nothing but a pair of tighty-whities. We both burst into laughter.

"What the hell is he doing?" I said to Billy.

"I have no clue but Jason sounded wasted on the phone." We pulled up to the edge of the creek and got out of the truck.

"What are you doing, Kyle?" Billy yelled at him.

"What the fuck does it look like? I'm trying to get us out of here!" He shot back.

"Okay, but why are you naked?" Billy yelled.

"It's like six degrees out here, I didn't want to get fucking hypothermia, you prick." Kyle jousted before suddenly losing his balance. He swayed back and forth but his intoxication was no match for gravity and he fell into the creek with a splash.

We hurled into a fit of laughter as Kyle angrily got back onto his feet.

"Get over here and pull us out!" he demanded.

I squinted to get a better focus on the inside of the truck. I could see Jason and Darryl sitting on the bench seat, topless. "Billy!" I laughed, pointing toward the truck. "They're all naked!" He shifted his gaze from Kyle toward the cab of the motionless truck. He began to howl.

Billy walked around the cab of his truck. He reached for a pair of fishing waders and quickly climbed into them. He made his way across the creek to evaluate the situation. The water was about knee-deep. As he reached Kyle's truck, I watched him poke his head into the passenger window to say hi to Jason and Darryl. He cocked his head back and began laughing hysterically. He walked around the truck to where Kyle was waiting. Kyle pointed to the front wheel. Billy quickly assessed the problem before he said something else to Kyle and started back across the creek.

"So, Darryl is passed out and Jason is completely wasted. They're both in their underwear. I guess they were trying to push the truck out earlier," he said to me as he emerged from the cold water. We laughed as we climbed back into the truck. Billy slowly drove across the creek, careful not to pop a tire. Once we were close but not deep enough to flood the engine, he jumped out and grabbed a rope from the back seat. He attached the rope to his front hitch and walked over to attach the other end to Kyle's front hitch. Kyle quickly slid back into the driver's seat of his truck and started the engine as Billy made his way back. He hopped into the truck and slowly started to back up. Once the rope was fully extended, there was a slight tug before Kyle's truck started moving forward. Kyle stuck his thumb out the window and Billy stopped. He opened his door and stepped out into the water to detach the rope from both ends before we backed up out of the river. Once the boys made it out of the water, Kyle stumbled out of his truck and put his pants on. Jason left Darryl passed out and began to crawl out the passenger side, only he slipped on a rock on his way out. He fell next to the truck with a thud. We all laughed.

"Jason, you moron, pull it together." Kyle joked.

"Shut the fuck up and throw me my pants," Jason snapped back. Billy and I giggled. Kyle tossed us a beer. "Thanks a lot, you guys. We called about a million people and no one would come help us. I thought I was going to be sleeping naked next to these two idiots for the night," he said.

On our way back into town, Billy asked if I wanted to join him for a hot tub at his place. I asked if we could stop by my house so I could grab my bathing suit. He flashed me a devious smile as we drove past the turn off to my street.

We were fooling around in Billy's bedroom when my phone rang around 4 AM. But I just let it ring, I knew who it was. It rang again, and again. Finally, I got out of his bed and answered it. I didn't even get through the first syllable of "hello" before my mother's screams echoed through the speaker.

"Where the hell are you, Jordan?" I could feel her hands around my throat as she continued to yell.

She finally took a breath and I used the break to respond. "I'm at Billy's. I came over to watch a movie and we passed out on the couch. I'm sorry. He's driving me home right now." It was a lie, but it was the best half-truth I could come up with that would only make her hate him for a little while, instead of forever.

"You have five minutes to get home, I'll meet you there."

Click.

Billy and I jumped into our clothes and flew out the door.

When we pulled into the driveway, my mom was standing in the front window waiting with her arms crossed. I quickly said goodbye to Billy and jumped out of the truck.

I walked through the front door and she met me in the entrance, "What do you have to say for yourself?"

"I'm sorry?" I said sarcastically.

"Don't push me, Jordan. It's not like you to sneak out past curfew. What's going on?"

"I wanted to watch a movie," I shrugged.

I was grounded from seeing him for a week. But oddly, I did receive an extension on my curfew.

* * *

Billy left town for a few days at the beginning of December. During this time, I attended a Christmas party at a coworker's house. The gathering was a sloppy mess of degenerates, ranging from high school students to people in their late 20s, because in a town of 8000 people, when there's a party, the entire village attends. Back then we were too young to be picky about what we wanted to drink so we were stuck with whatever the bootlegger chose. There was no such thing as a tame night. We were animals. If a drink fell onto the floor, someone would crouch down and lap it up.

Around midnight I made my way down the hallway and ducked into a bedroom to call Billy. As we were saying goodbye, Mickey walked in. I didn't know he was even at the party, so he took me by surprise. By this time, we'd become friends again. Or so I thought.

He moved towards me, backing me into a corner. As I stumbled into two closet doors, almost knocking them off their track, he decided to break the hilarious news that he wanted to get back together. After laughing out loud, I politely told him I was seeing someone else and wasn't interested. He wasn't overjoyed with that answer. So, in an awkwardly grand gesture, he grabbed my arm and pulled me towards him, forcing me into a kiss that I think was supposed to be romantic, in a cheesy teen-movie kind of way. But it definitely fell short of the mark.

I pulled back and smacked him hard on the left temple.

Billy's friend Jake passed by the bedroom door at the exact moment I angrily pushed Mickey away. Concerned, Jake took a step backwards and entered the room. "Is there a problem here?" he asked. Jake was always the hero.

"It's okay. I have it under control," I responded.

Jake ignored me as he burned a hole through Mickey. "Take a hike, kid," he threatened.

Mickey looked from Jake to me and huffed a mature "Fuck you" before exiting the room.

"You okay?" Jake asked.

"Oh yeah, I'm fine. Case of the ex." I snickered. He laughed and we headed back to the party.

An hour later, I was standing outside gossiping with a few of the older girls from work, when one of them lit a joint. It slowly moved around the circle before it was handed to me. The group watched as I stared uncomfortably at the tightly rolled drumstick. I'd never smoked weed before and I really wasn't interested, but much like that time I licked a banana slug, peer pressure got the best of me.

Before long, I was loosely stumbling around the party drunk and high. No one explained the consequence of mixing the two.

When my curfew rolled around, I was beyond inebriated. I was slurring my words and stumbling all over the place. At one point, I caught a glimpse of the stove clock while pouring myself some gross cocktail from beyond the handbook. It was almost midnight. PM. I panicked, racing to the front door to put my shoes on. As I was slipping my left foot into the heel of my stiletto, I fell over. Jake laughed witnessing the tragic, hot mess from a short distance. I looked up at him from the floor and gave him a condescending smile. "Don't just stand there," I snapped as I reached for aid.

Jake, the hero he was, walked me home.

As we approached my front door, he turned to me and said, "You know, I wouldn't tell Billy about what happened with Mickey tonight. He'll lose his mind. Mickey was just drunk."

I knew he was right. I nodded and said goodnight.

Once I reached my bedroom, I tore my clothes off and threw them into a heap on the floor before drunkenly flopping onto my bed. I heard my parents' bedroom door creak open.

My mother called into the hallway, "Jordan? Is that you?"

"Yep, I'm home. Goodnight!" I called back.

"Night, kiddo," she slurred as she closed her bedroom door. I could tell she'd had a few drinks.

I quickly passed out.

I woke up the next morning to the sweet misery of a beastly headache. Every inch of my body pounded as I slowly and painfully shifted between the sheets. I was sweating and my heart was racing. I had a sick feeling in my stomach, not from the hangover, but from a horrifying dream I had. I'd dreamed that Mickey had snuck into my house, climbed on top of me in my drunken state and brazenly had sex with me. As a massive wave of nausea loomed over me, I rolled over to vomit into the trashcan next to my bed. I opened my eyes when the heaving was done and to my horror, I saw an empty condom wrapper on the floor next to the vomit-filled trashcan. I puked again. This time more violently than I'd ever puked before. And then I cried. And cried some more.

I spent all day Saturday hiding in my bedroom. I was filled with shame and regret. I'd lost my virginity to my loser ex-boyfriend under a circumstance that I couldn't even explain. I didn't know if I had let him in or if he snuck in through the back door. I couldn't remember anything. I just kept experiencing flashbacks of him on top of me sweating and thrusting. This wasn't how I pictured losing my virginity. It was supposed to be special, or at the very least memorable. A memory that future, tipsy, 60-year-old, permanent-vacation me would share with college kids at tiki bars desperately seeking wisdom on spring break.

* * *

Billy had moved out of his parents' house that winter and into a bachelor pad with Jake and Ethan. The boys had planned a Christmas Eve party and Billy confirmed that he would be by to pick me up around seven that night.

He showed up right on time. My mother and her best friend, Lauren, were drinking wine in the bar room, anxiously waiting to meet Billy for the first time. Up until this point, I'd sort of kept him away from her in fear that she would berate him about the night I snuck out. When the doorbell rang, they scrambled to answer it.

As I made my way toward the entrance, the two of them came flying around the corner from the kitchen, basically trampling over me to get to the door. They simultaneously stuck their hands out to greet Billy. My mother looked at him intently and looked back at me, then back to him, "Well aren't you just a sight for sore eyes." She couldn't contain herself. I rolled my eyes.

He smiled back at her and laughed. "Well, thank you," he said charmingly. I rolled my eyes again.

"Why don't you two join us for a drink before you leave?" Lauren blurted.

"Oh yes! I love that idea," my mother shouted. They were fawning over him like a couple of giddy schoolgirls.

Billy could sense my embarrassment as I shrugged from behind the Bobbsey twins. "It would be rude not to," he responded without missing a beat. I smiled, pleased with his sportsmanship. They beamed with excitement. They might as well have frantically jumped up and down, clapping like monkeys begging for a banana. And for the third time, I rolled my eyes.

We enjoyed a few glasses of wine while they flirtatiously interrogated my boyfriend. He eventually excused himself to use the bathroom. Or to search for a rope to hang himself, I'll never be sure. As we heard him close the bathroom door on the other side of the house, my mother looked at me, "I would have snuck out for him to," she said without wasting any time. "Doesn't make it right, but Jesus Christ, he is a handsome man."

Lauren giggled. "Nice work, kiddo."

Billy returned and we finished our wine before saying goodbye.

As Billy's party started to unwind later that evening, the guests, including his roommates, made their way down to the local watering hole. I'd started to clean up the kitchen when Billy grabbed my hand and led me down the hall into his room. As soon as the door closed behind us, we began to thrash around the room in a wild drunken frenzy. Clothes flew around the room as we ping-ponged from corner to corner. Before long, we were both completely naked on the bed, doing what *Degrassi High* always warned us about.

He suddenly stopped and looked at me. "Should we stop?" he asked.

Why do men do this? Should we stop? It's kind of too late for delusions of grandeur, don't you think? You've basically turned my insides into mashed potatoes at this point. It's safe to say that whatever you have, I now have. A noble gesture would have been putting on a condom, Don Juan.

When I shook my head in response to his ridiculous question, he leaned in and whispered, "I love you" like a true expert. And like the naïve kid that I was, I fell in love with him for it.

* * *

Our relationship blossomed with the seasons. As winter fizzled and spring flourished, Billy's adventurous nature left no room for dullness. He would show up on his motorcycle to pick me up from school. All my friends would watch in awe as he whisked me away for long rides down old highways that lead to beautiful restaurants and ocean lookouts on mountain cliffs. We spent spring break in Tofino where he rented a cabin on the beach. As the temperature climbed, we occupied our weekends camping with his friends and weekdays swimming in the river. Every whim was wrapped inside a romantic gesture. It felt surreal. I was living in a romance novel. Not really on the level of Jane Austen, it was more of the Fabio-on-the-cover variety. Everything was good, so good that it felt too good to be true.

When summer shifted into gear, like most things that seem too good to be true, I learned that my relationship was, in fact, just so.

I started to hear rumors from his friends' girlfriends that Billy was seeing someone else. Ladysmith was a small town and I knew how much people loved to talk so I chose to disregard the gossip. The funny thing about gossip is that it usually stems from somewhere truthful. A little rumble may quickly turn into a raging avalanche, destroying everything in its path. But that tiny rumble that started the commotion holds weight.

Billy decided to go to Calgary for two weeks to visit his brother. He left me the keys to his truck while he was away because he hated my tiny, jellybean-colored deathtrap. My first car was a teal Turbo Firefly. The heater didn't work, the interior was covered in cigarette burns, and the tires were so bald that driving around in the rain felt like you were playing Mario Kart on a coke bender. On top of all that, my dad had a mechanic friend remove the turbo because he wasn't overly thrilled with my lead foot. The heap could barely hit 90 clicks an hour or make it up hills without stalling. It was the antipode of safety and reliability. It was like driving around the pullout method.

Billy called me one afternoon with the news that Josh, a friend from out of town, was coming to visit and he would be staying at his place. His roommates were away on a fishing trip so he asked me to meet Josh at the house to let him in and give him the spare key.

I arrived to find Jake in the kitchen, heating up leftovers in the microwave. "Oh, hi!" I said, surprised as I entered through the back door. "I wasn't expecting anyone to be here. Billy said you guys were fishing."

"Yeah, we just got back this morning," he said. "What's up? Why are you here?"

"Apparently Josh is going to be sleeping on the couch for a little while. Billy asked me to drop off the spare," I responded.

"Oh. Well, I haven't seen him yet," he said as the microwave beeped and he reached inside to grab his plate.

"Okay, I'll just leave it with you then," I replied. I looked at him curiously. Jake and I had become close over the past few months. I was about to turn and leave as a bout of adrenaline rushed through me. I started again, "Jake? Can I ask you something that stays between us?"

He looked at me. He knew what I was about to ask. He chewed awkwardly as he stuttered, "Uh, sure, what's up?"

"There's a rumor floating around that Billy's seeing someone else. Do you know anything about that? Has he brought anyone else here?" I asked him.

He swallowed the lump of food he'd been chewing. "Uh, not that I know of, no," he said and quickly looked away.

"Jake." I begged.

His eyes darted around the room before resting back on me, "This is a really uncomfortable situation for me, you know I love you, we're friends, but he's my friend too. I just..."

"So, it's true then?" He had admitted by default. I wasn't stupid. I knew the answer before I even asked the question. I just needed to hear it from someone who wasn't a gossiping bimbo. "Who is she? Please just be honest with me, I promise no one will know it came from you."

He stared at me for a minute and finally gave in. "Her name is Jane. She's from Victoria."

My stomach jumped up through my chest and into my throat. I couldn't breathe. I tried to hold back my tears. I threw the house key on the table and flew out the back door in a fit of anger and heartache.

I went for a long drive. My cellphone rang as tears streamed down my face. I looked down at the ringing phone and saw Billy's name light up on the screen. I didn't answer. He called back. I didn't answer. It rang a third time and I finally answered it, "What?"

"Did I catch you at a bad time?" He asked.

"Yes. What do you want?" I fired at him.

"I was just calling to see if you'd met with Josh yet, but if this is a bad time I can call back later," he replied.

I paused. "Who the fuck is Jane and why are you doing this to me?" I shot from the hip, unable to suspend my anger.

Silence fell over the phone for a second before he started in. "She's a friend of mine from Victoria, why?"

"A friend? Really? Don't fucking lie to me," I yelled into my cell phone as my tears blurred my vision of the road ahead.

"Yes, a friend. Why? Who have you been talking to?"

I didn't want to throw Jake under the bus, so I blamed the girls. They were the obvious scapegoat. Billy spent the next 30 minutes reassuring me that he and Jane were just friends. He told me his sister-in-law cut her hair, so Jane would pop by the house for a drink afterwards to catch up. I knew he was lying but I loved him. I didn't technically have proof that he was seeing her romantically, so I used that assessment to justify my naïveté. I made a decision in that moment that I would fight for him. Because cheaters are always worth fighting for, said every idiot ever.

* * *

One afternoon, not too long after that, Billy asked me to come to his baseball game. He was on a local beer league team and they were hosting a tournament in town. I had to decline because I was scheduled to work that day. I also had to decline because the idea of watching amateur baseball was about as exciting as the prospect of bathing my grandfather.

I'd recently started working at a local coffee shop. Being new to the job, I didn't feel comfortable asking for the day off, but when the boss showed up early to do paperwork, he offered to finish the day and close up. So I decided to stop by the field and catch the end of the game.

When I arrived, the gossip queens were huddled together on a bench. I looked around in the desperate hope of seeing someone, anyone, else I knew, but I didn't recognize a single face. I took a deep breath and began to stride toward my doom. As I neared the group, Caroline spun around making eye contact with me. Her eyes widened before she turned and whispered to the gaggle. Then simultaneously, they all looked over and waved like the creepy valley girl collective they were. Call me Sherlock, but something was up.

When I approached the pity-party, Tara greeted me. "Hey! Billy said you weren't able to make it today."

"I finished early," I said as I sat down. I peered onto the field as Billy was jogging toward the dugout. When he glanced in my direction, he looked surprised to see me. "Who's winning?" I asked the girls.

Tara looked at me, ignoring my question. Then she blurted, "Billy invited Jane. She's sitting over there with his parents." She pointed across the field. I followed the length of her arm, past the tip of her finger and squinted into the distance. She was pointing at a petite brunette girl sitting on a lawn chair next to Billy's mom.

"So?" I replied. "They're friends."

Caroline rolled her eyes. "Seriously? You can't be that gullible."

Yes actually, I CAN be that gullible, you goddamn twat, I'm 17. I mean, that's probably what I wanted to say. I didn't though because, you know, social suicide.

I watched Jane across the field. She was cool and comfortable around his family. I knew that despite the girls' horrible track record, they weren't making any of this up. The background noise faded and all the walls I'd built up came crumbling down around me. I could feel my eye sockets begin to well with tears. I stood up and ran toward the parking lot. I quickly started my car and turned my head around to watch behind me as I backed out.

I suddenly heard a pounding on the driver's side window. "ROLL DOWN THE WINDOW!" Billy yelled. I slammed my foot on the brake. My heart was racing as I glared at him through the glass. I looked at him, then to her in the far distance, before resting back on him. Disappointed, I shook my head. And without warning, I peeled out and sped off.

I just drove. I drove until I almost ran out of gas. I stopped at a gas station to fill up and bought a pack of cigarettes. I wasn't a smoker, but I felt like it was a good time to start killing myself. I drove around for three hours, smoking, coughing and listening to loud, somber music. How did I wind up here? And when did I become so emo?

As night rolled in over the mountains and darkness engulfed our tiny town, I decided to stop by Billy's house and pick up my belongings. Because what would be a better, less dramatic time than after I'd been crying for hours?

When I turned onto his street, I noticed a black Acura parked in his driveway. I knew it was Jane's car. Billy noticed me pull up from the kitchen window and came bolting out the back door. He approached my car just in time to stop me from getting out of it and reigning sweet unmerciful hell.

"What are you doing here?" he asked. I looked up and saw Jane appear in the kitchen window. I transferred my gaze back to him.

"She's here? Are you fucking kidding me?" I fired at him. "I came to get my shit, because I don't want to see you again after today." I glared at him with all the hatred I could muster. I huffed in frustration, closed my car door without saying a word and drove home.

Asshole Rating: 8.5 Hoarding girlfriends is only acceptable if you own a porn magazine, wear a housecoat every day and throw parties that Motley Crüe attends.

I poured through my front door and collapsed into my mother's arms. She escorted me into the bar room, where Lauren was waiting, and poured me a glass of wine.

"What's going on?" she asked.

I broke into a streamline of sobs and told them the entire story. It was hard for my mother to hear it. She really loved Billy, and I mean LOVED him, like she would have been totally okay with all three of us ending up on Maury because of some kind of incestual love triangle.

They struggled to listen through the echoes of sniffling and pouting and an hour and a bottle of wine later, the phone rang. I assumed it was Billy calling, so I asked my mom to answer it. She lifted the receiver to her ear. "Hello?" she answered as she looked over to me. There was a moment while she listened. "Yes she is, who's speaking?" her eyes widened as she looked at me. "One moment." She put her hand over the mouthpiece as she whispered across the bar to me, "It's Jane."

My heart stopped. I fumbled my glass of wine, nearly spilling it all over myself. I reached for the receiver and cleared my throat before answering. "Hello?"

"Hi Jordan, I think we need to talk." Her raspy, sex-hotline voice cracked from the other end. Like it wasn't enough that she was sleeping with my boyfriend she had to sound like a porn star while she was doing it. "Are you busy tonight? I was hoping we could do this in person."

It was the last thing I wanted to do, but I knew she was right. "I can cancel my plans." I lied.

"Okay. I'll be there in 45 minutes. Where do you live?"

I gave her my address while my mother and Lauren curiously listened. I said goodbye and hung up the phone.

"What the hell is going on?" Lauren asked.

I just stared at them for a minute, unsure what had just transpired. "Jane is coming here to talk, apparently," I responded.

They looked at me in shock. My mother stared at me in disbelief for a moment before piping in. "Well this is an extremely rare and mature approach. Good for you two!" She raised her glass, as if toasting to my misfortune.

I watched while her wine glass hung in the dead, awkward air before I disappeared to my bedroom to get ready. There was no goddamned way that I was going to look like a blobfish when the Disney princess showed up.

Jane arrived exactly 45 minutes later. My mother answered the door. I could hear her welcome Jane into the house from my room so I quickly pulled a shirt over my head. I gave myself a quick look in the mirror before I flung my bedroom door open. I was surprised to find my mother standing on the other side of the door.

She whispered to me, "Jordan, she looks exactly like you. I can't even believe it."

Annoyed, I brushed past her. I blazed around the corner from the hallway into the front entrance. And there she stood at a whopping, equal 5'2" and 115 pounds, with long brown hair that brushed against her lower back. She was a few years older than I was but we looked eerily similar. We just stood there, staring at each other, while my mother and Lauren watched with an imaginary bowl of popcorn. Neither of us said a word. As I watched her, I knew this went a lot deeper than I imagined. And I knew she was realizing the same thing. We'd been played. Hard.

"Why don't you girls join us for a glass of wine?" My mother suggested.

"You read my mind," Jane responded with a sigh of relief. The four of us made our way to the bar room. It was a hot summer night so we opened the French doors, allowing a soft breeze to fill the room. Lauren poured Jane a glass of wine as she nervously scanned the bar top. Noticing an ashtray, she looked over to my mother. "Mind if I smoke?"

"Not in the least," my mother responded. Everyone lit up, including myself. My mother gave me a look of disapproval as I inhaled. She watched me as I awkwardly exhaled, knowing that this was a new habit. But she didn't say a word. She understood what kind of potential cool-expulsion I was under.

Jane took a sip of her wine before addressing the elephant in the room. "Well, don't we look alike."

My mother and Lauren laughed. And like any good icebreaker, the confessional poured out of us, like a hit man and a rapist trapped in a room together on a sinking ship. It was as if we had to find personal salvation before our lungs filled with water and it was all over. As it turned out, Jane was with Billy in Calgary when I had his truck. They'd been seeing each other for over five months. What was most disturbing was how closely our individual relationships with him mimicked one another, right down to the name he called us in bed. He was collecting girlfriends like trophies.

After a bottle of wine and half a pack of cigarettes, we quit feeling sad or angry and slowly started to find the twisted humor in all of it.

"Let's go there," Jane proposed.

"To Billy's? Now?" I hesitated.

"Fuck him. We should confront that asshole," she said.

My mother and Lauren nodded their heads in agreement like this was some sort of *First Wives Club*. If Jane had said, "Let's go to his house and stab that fuckbag in the jugular!" I truly believe they would have complied. It's important to always have psychotic women in your corner. No matter how strong and independent you think you may be, you cannot drag a 180-pound body into the woods and bury it on your own. You're going to need help. But this isn't *The Serial Killer's Guide to Obscurity*. (Stay tuned for the next book.)

I agreed. I don't know why I agreed. Conflict wasn't really in my nature. But she was like a tiny, excited Napoleon Bonaparte. She'd recruited me for the Battle of Asshole Acre to avenge our dignity. I didn't know what she was capable of but I knew it would probably cause a lot of damage. She wielded me to march forth with her. Probably to our deaths.

So we charged with a vengeance. Right into her black Acura.

Billy's roommates were smoking weed on the porch when we pulled into the driveway. But as we both emerged from behind the elusiveness of Jane's tinted windows, they stopped in horror. With their jaws slung open, smoke billowed around them like they were in some kind of low budget rap music video.

A deceptive smile formed over Jake's lips. "Oh shit, this is going to be good," he said aloud, between hoots from the joint. I knew he wanted Billy to get caught.

"Where is he?" I asked the boys as we approached the front door.

Ethan casually took a drag before he responded. "He's in his room, helping Josh pack."

We walked through the front door. Jane was ahead of me so I followed her down the hallway toward Billy's room. She'd clearly been here before. When she walked through the bedroom door, Billy looked up at her and smiled, just before I appeared behind her. His smile quickly faded. Jane, high on adrenaline, stormed toward him. She reached back, almost whacking me in the face with the back of her palm. Then, like a slow-motion action sequence in a shitty soap opera, her arm flung forward with full force, and like the sound of close thunder, her open palm landed directly on Billy's left cheek. Before he had an opportunity to compute what was happening, she wound up and smacked him again. TWICE! I couldn't believe it. I was with Rambo. If Rambo had 350CC's pumped into each breast. "Fuck you!" she shouted at him. She started to scream at the top of her lungs.

Everything faded to a blur after that.

As I snapped back to reality, Billy looked past Jane, making eye contact with me. I backed into the doorway, glaring at him. I wiped the tears from the corners of my eyes before they were noticeable. He mouthed, "I'm sorry." But I was emotionally stunned as my glare matched her screams. I didn't say a word. I couldn't. Besides, she was saying enough for the both of us.

She finally took a breath and turned on her heel. She looked at me before exiting the room. "Let's get the fuck out of here!"

Jane had singlehandedly changed my opinion of myself. I suddenly felt like a pushover. Was this how women were supposed to respond to situations like these? Was hitting Billy acceptable behavior? Are you supposed to slap the ever-loving shit out of someone for cheating on you? I was clearly out of the loop here.

We hopped back into Jane's car and sped off, ripping a patch out of the lawn like we were driving the General Lee.

"Where now?" I asked.

"Smoke a joint at the beach?"

I wasn't sure if this was a question or a statement. But it certainly was crazy. I wanted to go home and crawl into bed, but I didn't want to leave Jane. I didn't want her to go back to him. I feared that if I left her alone, she would cave. We had to hold a united front. I didn't want her to have him. I didn't want him to have either of us. He deserved to suffer. But I knew from her spastic reaction, from her violent passion, that she was weak.

So I stuck it out. We hung out in her shitty 1994 Acura, smoking weed at the beach, ignoring our phones. It was a real *Thelma and Louise* moment. Well, minus the murder thing, and the cool outfits, and that whole ride or die friendship. Actually, I guess for them it was more of a ride AND die friendship. Okay, it was really nothing like *Thelma and Louise*.

Crazy Level: 6.9 However, this could have been worth an 7.9 if we'd made-out afterwards.

When she dropped me off at home, she said she would call me later that week to check in.

* * *

Jane didn't call me that week, or the week after. I eventually caught wind that she had gone back to Billy. I wasn't surprised.

And then one afternoon, she called.

"Hello?" I answered.

"Hey. It's Jane. I just wanted you to hear from me that Billy and I decided to work things out. It's for the best for us. We think we can get through this. I Just didn't want you to hear it from anyone else first," she said.

I sat quietly on the other end as I sunk into a better, quieter world. A world where people aren't interested in pop-country music or apologies from cheating fucknuggets.

"Hello?" she whispered.

I quickly spiraled back from Valhalla. "Hey man, good luck with all that," I responded with my most affluent sarcasm before hanging up the phone.

* * *

Summer faded and acceptance surfaced as I was about to begin my senior year. By that point, I just wanted to get through grade 12 and get out of that town. I made the decision when the school year started that I would condense my workload into one single semester to graduate in January rather than June.

Billy called me around the end of September. I hadn't heard from him in over a month. I answered right away. I suppose I missed him. I suppose I was lonely. I suppose I was 17 and still wanted to win.

He told me things weren't working out with Jane. I knew he'd moved her in, because for the last month I'd gone out of my way to drive past his house on my way to AND from school every day and her car was always parked in the driveway.

Crazy Level: 6.2 Once crazy hits a highpoint, like a 6.9, it takes time to drop again. You have to put in a lot of non-crazy deeds to prove you can be responsible with your lunacy. Stalking your ex-boyfriend's house is not exactly one of those non-crazy deeds.

He told me that he was going to Calgary to see his brother for the week. He asked if I would meet him in Vancouver the following Friday and spend the weekend in the city. By this time, my mother was going through her separation with my dad so all the rules had sort of flown out the window. She had no objections when I informed her of my plans. In fact, I don't think she even asked me where I was staying. We were both depressed over our breakups and we didn't know what to do with each other. So we just sort of coexisted in separate worlds.

I took the weekend off and caught a ferry to Vancouver that Friday evening. I arrived at the hotel before Billy. With the room under his name, I wasn't able to check in without him, so I sat at the hotel bar and ordered myself a drink. By this time, I'd spent a few years barhopping with a fake ID. The photo looked nothing like me but my assertion and confidence were undeniable. Most of the time I wasn't even asked for identification.

After a short while, I felt a tap on my shoulder. "Are you old enough to be here, Miss?" A deep voice probed from behind me.

I swung around, ready to fight—for my right to party. But I was surprised to find Billy. I laughed. And like no time had passed at all, I threw my arms around him.

Once we checked in, we decided to relax and call for room service before heading out for the night. I hopped into the shower as Billy scanned through the menu.

I'd just finished straightening my hair when I heard a knock at the door. I stood in front of the mirror in a fluffy, white hotel robe as I applied a dab of hairspray and touched up my mascara.

When I emerged from the bathroom, the room was dimly lit. Our room service was arranged on the small hotel room table next to a giant window overlooking the city. Billy lit a candle and pulled out a chair. He motioned for me to sit down.

"Maybe I should get dressed," I said. Romance made me uncomfortable.

"You look perfect and I'm starving," he responded.

We ate dinner, drank wine and pretended not to feel our guilt. As we finished, I looked out to the city. I felt a sense of comfort. A part of me wished I were alone in that hotel room. Alone in that city. Billy watched me intently. My gaze shifted back to him. He motioned for me to come around to his side of the table. When I stood up and moved closer to him, he pulled me onto his lap.

"I'm kicking her out. This is it. I'm finished and I really want you to consider giving me a chance to make things better again. You don't have to answer now. Let's enjoy this weekend but I just wanted you to know that." Then he kissed me for the first time in months and everything fell away. My sadness, my anger, my loneliness it all disintegrated into nothing. He carefully stood up and untied my robe. With my back against the wall-length window on the 17th floor of that city hotel, we made up. Twice.

* * *

After our weekend getaway, I didn't hear from Billy for days. I assumed he was busy dealing with his breakup. On Saturday, I received a text message from Jane (in fact this was the first text message I'd ever received, ever). It read: "*Jordan, I found the hotel receipt. I hope you had a nice weekend with my boyfriend.*" I didn't respond. I called Billy instead. He didn't answer.

He called me back that night. I answered the call on the first ring. "What is going on? I thought you said you were kicking her out?" I yelled without greeting him.

"Things are messy right now. She can't just move out, she has nowhere to go. She's staying here until she figures everything out," he responded. I don't know why I bought it, but I did. If Billy's lies were for sale, he could have bought a beach house in Malibu with the income he'd have made from my reliable patronage.

Days turned into weeks, weeks turned into months and still nothing had changed. Jane was still at the house, Billy was still making excuses and we were still sneaking around to see each other. Eventually, I chose to see the bigger picture. He was lying. Jane wasn't going anywhere. He wanted the best of both worlds and he was taking them. Depression set in. I was skipping school all the time. I wasn't going to be able to graduate early at this rate. I'd already been forced to drop biology and chemistry due to poor attendance.

One night at the local pub, I ran into Billy's friend, Ian. We flirted, he bought a few rounds and then, like any 17-year-old desperate for revenge, I went home with him.

I was a train wreck. Undeterred by the terrible sex, I continued seeing Ian out of spite. When Billy caught wind that I was sleeping with him, he lost his mind. I didn't care. Fuck him. If he was going to play his game, I would play my own.

* * *

Winter reared its dreary head, Christmas came and went and my grades had continued to slip. I was in a tough position. With exams a month away, I was four credits short of being able to graduate in the first semester like I had planned.

One afternoon I was called into the office. Upon entering the small room, I was greeted by the principal, my counselor, and Mr. Farley, one of the aid teachers whom I'd been close with since grade nine.

Mr. Farley smiled nervously before he spoke. "I called this meeting," he stated as he fidgeted with his coffee mug. "We know how badly you want to get out of here. And we have no intention of keeping you in a place where you are clearly unhappy. But we also don't want to watch you waste your potential. You deserve to graduate. Up until this year you've been a good student."

The principal continued. "We've been presented with a new program worth four credits." He looked at me with conviction. "The four credits that you are currently missing. It's new to our curriculum and we are going to test-drive it on you, if you are willing."

My counselor piped in. "You will have to create a career portfolio. For someone like you, it shouldn't take longer than a weekend." He smiled encouragingly. "So study for your exams, ace them, create this portfolio, and Bob's your uncle."

Tears streamed down my cheeks as I realized what these three men were doing for me. I forced a smile and thanked them for understanding before I stood up to leave.

Mr. Farley followed me out of the office. He closed the door behind him and lowered his voice to a whisper. "Jordan can I offer you a little bit of advice?"

I wiped a lone tear from my right cheekbone and nodded receptively.

"Get out of this town." He paused to allow it to sink in before he continued. "Travel, do whatever you have to do to not get sucked into the bullshit that swarms this place. Ladysmith is not for you and no boy is worth the rest of your life." He smiled and before I could respond, he walked away.

* * *

A week after exams, I was on a plane to Switzerland and I hadn't talked to Billy in over three weeks. I spent a few months living in Bern and traveling around the Toblerone capital. It felt good to breathe new air. I woke up early every day, went out for coffee, and wandered around the city. I'd take the train to other towns just for fun. I went to museums, galleries, and libraries just to pass the days. I spent hours on grassy knolls drinking wine and writing. I was alone, far away from everyone. And for the first time, I felt right with myself.

I received an email from Billy in my last week. He wanted me to know that Jane was moving out and that he hoped we could work things out. I never replied.

I returned home just before graduation and prom. I hadn't planned to take part in either, but my mother talked me out of being an asshole with her highly original speech about missing 100% of the shots you don't take. I think the moral of that quote was always a little lost on her but in Canada, you aren't making a point unless it's with a hockey hero.

After my graduation ceremony, a swarm of graduates and their families spilled out the front entrance. As the herd thinned out, I noticed Billy in the distant parking lot, standing next to his truck. I looked at my mother as she stared off in his direction. Her gaze shifted to me. She sighed. "I'll meet you back at the house."

Bloody enabler.

I slowly made my way toward Billy. As I approached him, I saw someone I hadn't seen before. He'd changed. He was thin and exhausted. I looked at him for a long minute then, without saying a word, I climbed into the passenger side of his truck and we drove off.

We sat facing the beach in silence, staring out the windshield for what felt like the lifespan of honey. He looked over to me, desperate for a response. And then something very uncomfortable happened. He started to cry. I didn't know what to do. I've never known how to react when people cry in front of me. Can't they call a hotline or cry alone in the comfort of their own shower like normal sad people? A part of me knows that the right thing to do is to hug that person, but I just don't want to and I'm sure people are capable of sensing a disingenuous embrace. This has left me to live with an irrational fear of being known as an awkward hugger. So as a general rule, I try not to hug anyone when I'm sober.

"What have I done? You're a different person," he finally spewed between light sobs.

"I don't know," I said as I continued to stare at the ocean. "I can't keep spinning in circles around you. I don't want this life anymore."

"So is that it? Can't I fix it somehow? I want to make this work with you," he begged.

"I can't trust you. What makes this time different?"

"Let me prove it to you. Give me a chance to build a friendship and prove myself," he said through tears.

I sat silently for a while, considering his proposal. I finally looked back to him. He was a broken man. He cowered helplessly. I couldn't turn on him. I felt sorry for him. And I still loved him, despite knowing I shouldn't. "Okay. Let's work at a friendship. If you can change my mind, I'll give you another chance. But this is it. Fuck this up and I'll burn your house down," I said semi-sarcastically.

He looked up at me with his big, stupid, sorrowful eyes and I swear an evil twinkle passed through them.

* * *

We spent the next few weeks enjoying summer together. I enrolled myself at the university in Nanaimo so I could be close to him. My love for him was like a switch, one that needed to be violently pulled out of the wall, unwired, and bricked over.

Around the end of July, we were invited to a friend's birthday party. It was a typical small-town bash. Everyone drank together and took smoke breaks together, a select few even snorted rails together. Fair to say, I've been to better parties. The flailing birthday girl decided she wanted to go to a club in Nanaimo. I recently lost my fake ID so I was unable to go but I told Billy it was fine if he wanted to. I wish I could say he hesitated, but he practically trampled over me to ride shotgun.

A few of us stayed behind and continued drinking at the house. About an hour and a half later, Sonja's phone rang. When she answered the call, loud laughter echoed from the speaker. It was Caroline, drunk, calling from the club. Sonja looked over to me as the conversation went on in her ear. She glanced at the floor before she hung up.

"What's up?" I asked her.

"Oh, nothing. They're all wasted," she responded without making eye contact.

"Okay, something's up," I pushed before it suddenly clicked. "What did he do?"

"Please don't shoot the messenger." She took a deep breath. "Jane was there and apparently they've left together." My whole body went numb. I stared down at my hands, confused by the cold sensation. "Are you okay?" she asked.

I snapped out of it. "Would you be?" I fired at her. "I knew I couldn't trust him. What the fuck is wrong with me?" I pulled my cell phone from my purse and dialed his number. No answer. I called again. No answer. I called again, still no answer. I called again, and again, and again. I probably called him 50 times. He never picked up. I went home.

I curled up in bed and continued to call Billy between fits of hyper-ventilating sobs. By this time, it was probably 2 AM. I had nearly cried myself into exhaustion. I called him one last time and finally on the 5th ring, someone picked up.

"Hello?" a girl's voice answered.

"What the fuck is going on? Where 's Billy?" I screamed into the receiver.

"He's asleep Jordan. Stop calling." The line went dead. I called back. No answer.

Asshole Rating: 8.0 This rating dropped because at this point, his behavior was to be expected. I'm not totally sure if I believe the old adage "once a cheater, always a cheater" but I think it's safe to say that Billy would never be responsible for changing anyone's mind.

My fury took on a life of its own. I knew I wouldn't be able to sleep. I reached into my nightstand where I kept an emergency pack of cigarettes. I knew I was too drunk to drive but I didn't care. I had to get out of that house before I lost my mind. I grabbed my keys off the kitchen table and flew out the door.

I drove. I drove all over town before I decided that I had to get out of town. The town I once loved had become this dark stain on my unbridled adolescence. My music was blaring. I guess between that and my traumatized headspace, I hadn't realized that I'd wound up on the Malahat. The highway was dark, wet, empty and I felt lifeless. I pulled over, onto a cliff-side viewpoint. The lookout was high on the mountainside and towered over the seemingly endless ocean. I got out of my car and walked over to the railing. I looked out over the edge. I felt a surge of self-awareness as the 100-meter drop came into focus. I could faintly hear the waves crash against the rocks below. I climbed onto the railing and sat there. I smoked and I smoked as the rain rapped against my numb forehead. The summer breeze flirted against my skin while I considered how easy it would be to push myself off the railing and into the dark, endless abyss below. I thought about how much it would hurt for that millisecond as my cranium smashed into the rocks before it was all over. I winced.

I sat there for hours. Smoking. I smoked the entire pack of cigarettes before I realized the rain had stopped and the clouds had begun to part. The sun was going to come up soon. I lowered myself off the railing and walked back to my car. I looked at my cell phone sitting in the console. Seven missed calls. I flipped it open, hoping to see Billy's name appear under the Missed Call line. None of them were from him.

I started the engine and decided to make my way back home. The Malahat is a dark, dangerous highway nestled in the mountains of Vancouver Island. It winds and twists its narrow snake-like body around giant rocks, through tall trees and there is no barricade to separate you from oncoming traffic. It was still pitch black as my deathtrap careened down the highway, the trees shielding any light. I started to think about Billy again. I could hear Jane's voice in my head, telling me he was asleep. I hadn't realized that I'd begun to pick up speed. A set of high-placed headlights appeared ahead. I could tell it was a semi. The monster grew larger and more intimidating as it neared. I stared into its headlights. Everything went white. I turned the wheel slightly shifting my car into the semi's path. I closed my eyes and took my hands off the wheel, as I heard the horn's blare grow louder and louder. I suddenly opened my eyes into the vast brightness. The semi was coming full speed, trying to swerve out of the way. I froze and suddenly my car jerked hard to the right. I could hear the semi's horn blare as it ripped past me. I slammed on my breaks, stopping just inches from sinking my pint-sized Firefly into the ditch. I gasped for air. My heart was racing. The semi hadn't stopped. I burst into tears on the shoulder of the road. What the hell was wrong with me? I didn't want to die… did I?

* * *

I spent the rest of the summer drinking and partying with friends. I didn't speak to Billy but I heard he and Jane moved in together again. I wish I could say I was surprised.

One night at a party, I ran into Billy's brother Shane. He'd recently gone through a break-up and was in the same state of disarray I was. Like a predator, I pegged him from a mile away. I guess I was feeling particularly spiteful then because when he asked me to go for a walk with him, I practically jumped at the chance to initiate a small-town scandal.

The party was out in the sticks on a friend's ranch, so we started along a long dirt road. Shane opened up about his relationship and apologized for what his brother had done. Once we decided we were sad and pathetic enough to justify it, we kissed.

Listen, I realize that kissing Billy's brother was petty and low. I just didn't care. I was harboring so much resentment towards Billy that I hoped he found out. I wanted to hurt him, in the worst way possible. Forgiveness wasn't something I'd come to learn yet. I was 18. I still had a few allotted immature screw-ups in the bank.

Shane suggested that we go for a drive for a little privacy. Not-so-code for 'let's see how badly we can fuck this up.' We headed back to the house, toward his car, jumped in and quickly sped off before anyone noticed us leave together.

Once we were on the desolate, country road and away from the party, I climbed over the console and straddled him. We dry-humped like two drunk kids at a school dance, until he couldn't take it anymore. He pulled over to the side of the road and unzipped. I jumped off him into the passenger seat and leaned over the emergency break to give him head, but I guess he had other plans. He suddenly opened his car door and jumped out. He quickly made his way to the passenger side and pulled me out of the car. He picked me up and set me down on the hood of his car where we hate-fucked all of our sadness (and morals) away.

When we were finished, we returned back to our seats and he drove me home. We swore we would never speak to anyone about what had happened. Whoops (but the statute of limitations is definitely up by this point.)

Crazy Level: 7.9 I get a .1 deduction from Billy's asshole rating because while this was revenge, he started it.

* * *

The following week, I was slated to attend an introduction to Malaspina University and register for my classes.

As the tour ended, I found myself sitting with the guidance counselor in her office. She was going over classes and creating my potential schedule. She was talking so fast that the moment quickly sped up. Her words began to blur together. I stared into the distance behind her. Her voice grew long and drawn-out, as if it was spinning on a slowed-down record. I gazed up at the giant map of British Columbia that loomed over her head. I started to drift away from her. I closed my eyes and flashed back to Jane's open-handed crack against Billy's cheek, and the look in his eyes as he swung his head upright to look at me. Then my mind drifted to Shane and the hood of his car. What was I doing? I was about to repeat the last year of my life. I didn't travel all the way to Europe on a desperate search for my dignity just to wind up back here. "I've got to go!" I yelled as I stood up.

"I'm sorry?" the counselor said to me.

"I'm not ready for this. I have to think about it. Thank you for your time," I said as I ran out of her office. I ran down the hall and out the back door to the parking lot. I kept running. I ran until I reached the highway and when I got there I decided that I might as well just keep on running... and that's the story of how I wound up running across North America. Okay, no, that's the plot to Forrest Gump. But it would have been a good twist.

In reality I just ran to my car. When I collapsed into the driver's seat, I let out a long breath. I opened my eyes and saw my reflection in the rearview mirror. My skin was a dull mess. I was aged and exhausted. I barely recognized my own reflection.

When I arrived home, no one was there. I walked into the bar room and poured myself a glass of wine. I sat there, waiting until I heard the front door open.

"Jord?" my mother called through the house.

"In here," I yelled.

She appeared in the doorway. "What's up, kiddo?" she said softly, "How was orientation?" I was quiet. I realized I hadn't really talked to her all summer. She nestled in on the stool next to me and poured herself a glass of wine. "You ok?" She was concerned.

A tear fell down my cheek. I broke down into a million different pieces and told her everything. I told her what Billy had done. I told her about the semi truck and I told her about Shane. She stared back at me, without the disappointment I was expecting. Our sadness mimicking each other as we sat in silence.

"I can't stay here. I can't stay in this town and perpetuate this cycle. I feel completely lost. And I will never find myself again if I stay here."

She looked like she wanted to convince me otherwise, but she stopped herself. She slumped against the back of the barstool and took a long sip of wine. "You're probably right," she started, "I want you to stay on the path and go to school, but you'll just end up exactly where you were last year. Depressed and angry–wasting money on classes you'll never attend."

I couldn't believe she was agreeing with me. I was expecting a fight. "I'm sorry. I don't want to disappoint you, but I just can't do this anymore."

She nodded, "Well, where next then? Nanaimo? Victoria?" she asked.

"I don't think so," I shook my head, "I need to get off this rock. I've got some mending to do, and I want to do it where I can be a stranger."

She looked at me curiously.

Billy had taken a meat mallet to my heart and thrown it into the Pacific. I guess I decided to chase after it, "I'm going to Vancouver," I said. I was ready to be eaten alive by the city because no matter what shit Vancouver turned up, it couldn't be any worse than the crap-clogged creek I was currently submerged in. I felt like the forgotten puppy that Billy never wanted, roaming aimlessly in circles. My ability to trust was gone. I'd almost completely lost my mind... and my will to live.

She sunk deeper into the stool with a satisfied look on her face.

Honestly, it was probably for the best. Billy needed a taste of his own medicine and there's no way I could have taught him the lesson that his future wife did when she cheated on him... with a woman.

CHAPTER 3.5:
TOLERANCE

"I did not have sexual relations with that woman!"

—Bill Clinton, Liar

I learned many lessons between the fire and fury that I was dealt during my relationship with the Cheater. I learned it's important to weigh the consequences of your actions before your theatrical debut. I learned that people would say just about anything to deflect responsibility. I learned that in this life we can't afford illusions. We have to be able to accept defeat and realize when to cut the cord. I learned that manipulation was a parasite that preyed on the vulnerable. And I learned that sometimes to get what you want, you have to seize the opportunity to slap a motherfucker… twice.

The truth is, I felt wronged. I felt wronged by the Cheater and then wronged by Jane. I wanted both of them to experience the pain I experienced. That was what I wanted. But when you're blindly in love with someone, you go through waves of confusion and doubt. You don't want to believe that the love you're experiencing is the problem. You want to believe the cunt who is fucking up your love is the problem. Anyone who has experienced the entanglement of a love triangle understands the depth of malevolence. You will only truly wish death upon someone when they get in the way of your heart's desire and mouth hug your boyfriend's penis.

ALL MEN ARE ASSHOLES (...AND ALL WOMEN ARE CRAZY)

I would drive by the Cheater's house multiple times a day just to see Jane's car parked in the driveway. I knew it would be there. I wasn't doing it to see IF it was there, I was obsessively driving by just to see it, as though it was some kind of validation for my anger. I would fantasize about setting it on fire. I've never hated a car more than I hated that defenseless black Acura. I still cringe every time I see one. I couldn't control myself. I would ask mutual friends about Jane and the Cheater's relationship and when someone would mention that she was gaining weight or looked weathered or even just that she wore too much makeup, I felt satisfied. Like on some imaginary scale, I had won. I wanted her to get hit by a bus. I hated her. I hated her fake boobs. I hated her brown eyes. I hated her stupid car. I hated the town she grew up in. I hated whoever gave birth to her. I hated her smile. I hated the shitty nightclub she worked at. But most of all, I hated that Billy wanted her instead of me and that really, I didn't even hate her at all. I was jealous. And that jealousy was bubbling and oozing like a blister in the hot sun. Jealousy is the petri dish that cultures crazy.

When I started sleeping with Ian, I received a text message from Jane one night that read: "*Enjoy my sloppy seconds, slut.*" I can't remember if I responded but I feel the "slut" moniker was a tad unnecessary. I found out that Ian had dated Jane after the first time we slept together. He was terrible in bed. But I'll admit that once I found out they dated, I decided to keep sleeping with him because I wanted to hurt her, even if that meant sleeping with a turbo-douche who watched himself flex in his mirrored closet doors during sex. I just puked in my mouth reliving that.

You become self-destructive in love.

I was a child. I was introduced to psychotic behavior far too young and I didn't understand how I was supposed to tame the unwanted superpower. This type of manipulation is something most people don't encounter until adulthood, if ever. So I acted in the strangest and most corruptive way I knew how. I'd never lost like this before. I was naïve, desperate and in love with a fantasy. Was I a victim? Hell no. I made my choices. I knew the difference between right and wrong. But, in my defense, I was still a child. I wasn't even old enough to rent porn.

* * *

I remember when the Lewinsky scandal was introduced. It clogged up the news channels worse than the OJ trial. Everyone felt their opinions were notable and they had no problem dispelling them upon indifferent audiences. It was Lewinsky vomit, all over the place. I don't remember really having an opinion on the matter. I was only 12 when the story broke, but I remember my mother's opinion. I remember her saying that the president's affairs are private and have zero impact on his ability to lead the country. Not too tough to figure out whose side she was on (granted, this was before my father had cheated on her).

I originally wrote this chapter with reference to Bill and Hillary Clinton, four years ago. But now, after the most confusing upset since probably the fall of the Roman Empire, Donald Trump is the president of the United States and well, there's a new pussy-grabbing douche in town worthier of the slaughterhouse.

So was Monica Lewinsky a whore? Nah, it was 1998; if you didn't like sex, you were just weird. There. Case closed. Thank me later, America. Now, let's get down to political business, because what's a little satire if you're not docking dicks with politics?

This *Idiocracy*-themed world we're currently living in seems to have completely fallen off the rails. There is a shockingly substantial amount of people out there who, despite modern science, believe that the Earth is flat. The amount of followers you have dictates whether you can get published or not. A reality TV show host is the leader of the free world. And David Bowie is dead. We have fallen on weird, hard times. Surely, there is a salvation at the end of this apocalypse-inducing garbage heap? Surely.

Tumbleweeds.

Back to Donny, the guy who married an aging gold-digger, only to double back through divorce and marry a younger, more foreign gold-digger. You know, someone he could get blowjobs from while discussing covert ops and nuke codes over the phone, without worrying about breaking any privacy agreements.

What do we even know about this relationship, besides how terribly uncomfortable it is to watch on the news? Melania, are you still in there? Blink twice and scratch an H into the sand if you need rescuing. I mean, is she even human? Because I'm pretty sure it's the Terminator trapped in there.

What has happened in this woman's life that's lead her to become manipulated by a walking Cheeto? Mark my words, when the Trump administration ends, the Melania tell-all (ghostwritten) memoire about "how she became a pawn in the greatest game of chess when all she wanted was a sugar daddy" will emerge, moments after the divorce.

Now let's all join hands and sing together on our cloud of cream cheese while we remember how this crazy broad married the richest asshole she could find, in order to secure wealth and fortune. Melania Trump has to be crazy. She married for status and he married for a pat on the back from his creepy golf bros. Melania is someone who is driven by riches and Donny is someone who is driven by ego. You don't have to know Donald Trump to know the guy's an asshole. Just listen to him talk, you can hear how small his penis is. They truly deserve each other, unhappily forever after, just not anywhere near the Oval Office.

* * *

The Cheater opened me up to something I'd never known before him. I was malleable and he took advantage of that. I was stretched, tweaked and played with until I was molded into someone I eventually learned to hate. The Cheater wanted the best of both worlds. He wanted a mature relationship with someone close to his age and he wanted the adventure and fun his relationship with me allowed. Unfortunately, this manipulation took over my integrity. It took hold of everything I thought I stood for and left me a sloppy mess. I was putty in his hands.

I still have no idea what happened that night on the highway. I don't honestly think I wanted to die. I think my spirit was fractured enough that I wanted to give up. When you pour everything into someone for the first time, you don't expect that they're going to slap you in the face with it. You don't expect public ridicule and embarrassment. And you definitely don't expect that you're going to accept a half-assed apology and go running back, over and over again.

"Givers have to set limits because takers rarely do." —Irma Kurtz

The Cheater was a lying asshole. He used my naïveté to his advantage. I was young and impressionable and he knew he would be able to get away with shattering my heart because the odds of bouncing back are a lot higher the younger you are. He knew I could take his abuse, but at what cost? To what length would he have continued to take, had I continued to give?

Infidelity is a cruel bitch. It drives a person to madness. It takes over everything you've spent your entire life working towards and completely wipes it from the system. It changes you. It suffocates your trust and teaches you to assume the worst. You become a hollow cast of whoever you previously were, constantly searching for refilling. It pushes you so far past the outer limits that you usually end up recycling your experience because you can't unlearn that crazy.

The only thing I really had going for me was my youth. I was going to make more mistakes, but at least I was going to make them at a time when resilience was still a part of my makeup and alcohol was a food group. As if there's even an expiry on that theory.

I learned a lot of things from the Cheater, some things I'm thankful for, others I feel like I should send a compensation bill for. But most importantly, I've learned that you can't change people. However, if you're young and dumb enough, they sure can change you.

I look at my relationship with the Cheater as the budding of my insanity. He was where obsession began to burrow. Where infatuation took over morale. Where I began to lose control. Where that loss of control nearly ended my life and then, miraculously, saved it. It was the true beginning of a severely misguided womanhood, and Jesus Christ if I wasn't about to royally fuck shit up. Because, you'd think I would have learned the first time.

CHAPTER 4:
THE CODEPENDENT

"Everything is about sex, except sex. Sex is about power."

—Oscar Wilde

I met Richard on the set of Masters of Horror. He was tattooed, handsome and socially awkward. The perfect recipe for failure. A mutual friend introduced us—if you could even call him that. Let's just say, had we never been introduced, it wouldn't have been my worst missed connection, but hey I'm over it. Richard and I have swept the past under the rug and we've managed to salvage a friendship from the dust. By that I mean we exchange birthday wishes every year and I only sometimes imagine him mowing an active landmine.

When I moved to Vancouver, I stumbled effortlessly into the movie business. Okay, that's untrue. I was roped into background work by what can only be described as an extra's pimp through my roommate. I use the term pimp, because being an extra is about as desirable as blowing strangers in back alleys for employment. For anyone unfamiliar with movies, extras are essentially moving props that could easily be replaced with rolling sacks of potatoes that have little faces drawn on them. If you ever want to know what it feels like to be a leper in a busy grocery store, try background work. But don't mention that to Anthony, the 81-year-old professional extra who spends his final days on local sets, boasting of his glory days as a regular on The Love Boat.

One afternoon, I received an urgent call from my agent, frantically begging me to take an immediate gig. She told me the original girl they cast had bailed at the last minute and they needed a replacement. I had half an hour to get to set. She hung up the phone without divulging any details about the role or wardrobe. She barely managed to ramble off the location.

I arrived extremely unprepared but no one really seemed to care. When I announced myself at the extras sign-in table, the wrangler greeted me with an eye roll before begrudgingly searching for my name on the list. Once she found me, she shooed me off to makeup. Because that's the glamorous world of showbiz, folks.

As I made my way to the makeup trailer, I noticed my friend Dale moving around behind the set. I walked over to quickly say hello, but as I approached him, a grip cut in front of me to ask about a camera dolly. Dale began to answer him but retired mid-sentence when he recognized me. He reached around his coworker to give me a hug. We briefly caught up while the grip impatiently waited, loudly tapping his foot.

"Shit, sorry. Richard, this is Jordan," he briefly introduced us before his radio cut in and he had to run off.

Richard just looked at me. "So not that I really care, but how do you know Dale?" he asked as he fiddled with some equipment.

I rolled my eyes. "Well, not that I care to indulge you, but we grew up in the same miserable small town."

He stopped fidgeting with equipment and looked up at me. He half-smiled and for a minute it felt like the top of my skull had fallen off and he was looking at my exposed brain. "You're a weirdo," he said.

I didn't know if it was supposed to be a statement or an insult so I just glared at him.

"I probably wouldn't respond to that either. I grew up with Dale too. You must be from Ladysmith?" he said.

"Yeah," I responded.

"What's your name again?"

I huffed. "Jordan. And it was a total gas meeting you. Dick? That was your name, right?"

As I started to walk away he yelled after me. "My name is Richard!" Without turning around, I yelled back, "Whatever, Dick." I smiled to myself and kept on toward the makeup trailer.

* * *

A few days later I was running errands in Ladysmith while visiting my mother for the weekend. As I sprinted across the street to the pharmacy, a red, '73 convertible Impala nearly clipped me. I instinctually threw my middle finger in the air and continued to cross the street. The red car slowed down. "Jordan!" a voice came from the street just before I was about to walk into the pharmacy.

I looked up, annoyed. It was Richard. "Great. It must be my lucky day," I yelled at him as he crept by, slowing down the traffic behind him. His car crawled forward before disappearing around the corner. I was about to walk into the store but decided to wait a minute. The red boat circled around and appeared again. Richard pulled into an empty parking stall in front of the pharmacy. I rolled my eyes as he got out of the car. "So what? You're stalking me now?" I said to him.

"Maybe. Are you flattered?" he casually shot back.

"Not likely," I responded as he approached.

"So what are you doing?"

"What does it look like I'm doing?"

An awkward pause floated between us for a moment.

"Who hurt you?" he finally asked.

"Loaded question," I replied without missing a beat.

He laughed. "I'm heading to Nanaimo to check out a bookstore. Come with me. You look like you could use a drive," he said.

I looked at him resentfully. He was strange and that made me want to know more about him. "I don't know," I hesitated.

"I'm not a murderer. I really don't think a murderer would use a bookstore as bait."

I laughed, "Alright, why not?" So I hopped into the dream machine and off we sailed.

We cruised down the highway under the hot sun, 15 clicks over the speed limit, in comfortable silence. Richard was calm, confident, and he smelled like cigarettes and mistakes.

I turned to him to begin a dialogue but before I could say anything, something in my peripheral caught my attention. I looked to the back seat where a thick book openly rested, its pages flapping in the wind. I picked it up to read the cover, *The Art of War*.

Richard smiled at me and laughed, "What? You didn't think I could read?"

I looked at him, "Why are we going to a bookstore if you're hardly even through this?" I waved the book at him.

"You got me, the whole thing was just a ruse to get a pretty girl in my car. I'm taking you to Mexico, where I plan to sell you into a sex trafficking ring," he joked.

"Joke's on you, I'm not a girl," I said with a straight face. "But I have always wanted to go to Mexico."

We both laughed. He was sweet, in a weird way. I enjoyed him. I enjoyed his awkward company.

He dropped me off at home later that night and we exchanged numbers before parting ways.

* * *

Richard and I spent the next few weeks nonchalantly texting back and forth. It didn't really seem to be going anywhere until one night when I received a message from him asking what my plans were for the evening. I told him I was at a local pub having a drink. He didn't respond. But ten minutes later, he showed up. He joined me for a quick one before we decided to pick up a bottle of wine and make our way down to the beach.

We spent the evening sitting on the cold sand, exchanging old stories and secretly hoping we didn't get hemorrhoids. We laughed and drank and then laughed some more. We were like-minded and equally damaged, with the same dry sense of humor. When we finished the bottle of wine, we decided it was time to go. We got up and shook off all the sand before beginning the trek back to his car. As we strolled along the beach, I spotted a lifeguard tower. I ran towards it, because true to 19-year-old-drunk-girl fashion, I was always jumping at the chance to mount things that compromised my personal safety. When I approached the tower, I reached for the rails and one by one I climbed the steps, until I reached the top.

I positioned myself comfortably in the chair. Richard began to climb after me. As he reached the top, he grabbed onto my knee to steady his balance. And there we were, face to face, ten feet above the ground. We stared at each other for a lifetime before he reached behind my head, pulled me towards him and grazed my lips with his. He pulled back and laughed before moving in again to finish what he'd started.

We went back to his place that night.

* * *

A few months later I moved into Richard's apartment with him and his roommate because moving in right away is always a really great way to for a strong and lasting relationship. He lived above an alternator shop in a rundown building on a busy street. I didn't mind. Why would I? Previously, I was barely making rent at an apartment beyond my means on the beach. And by "barely" I mean I was surviving on pickles and ketchup, my mother was paying 85 percent of my bills, and I was about one drugstore makeup heist away from winding up on sugarbabies.com. Needless to say, my mother was thrilled that I was no longer going to be her financial burden.

I paid my rent by cooking and cleaning for them. It worked out for everyone. At least I like to tell myself that. I managed to convert their bachelor pad into a comfortable living space. Richard had two cars, so even when he was at work, I had a vehicle to get around in. I worked on set here and there, but not often. I didn't really have to. I was basically a stay-at-home mom for two grown men who probably wanted nothing less than to live with their mothers. It was a backwards *Three's Company*, except the erotic-fantasy version where Jack (me) was actually banging Chrissy (Rich) while Janet (Steve) jerked off in the corner. And our landlord was a polite Ethiopian man, rather than a nosey creep with a concerning disdain for his wife.

Richard would spend his nights playing guitar and making music on Garage Band as I sat on his bed in his plaid shirts, writing poetry. He introduced me to obscure bands I'd never heard of while we aimlessly drove around town in his Impala. We were basically hipsters before the term hipster had streamlined. Once in a while he would upload a song he wrote onto my iPod and I would write the lyrics while I was on set or doing promotional work on some golf course. Promotional work is code for being scantily clad while pouring shots of whatever alcohol you're promoting, as middle-aged, married men toss cringe-worthy sexual innuendos at you. But in fear of losing your gig, you just bite your tongue and laugh sweetly while you daydream about stabbing them in the femur with your corkscrew.

We had a good thing worked out. We were the same person. We respected each other's space and enjoyed each other's company at the same time. We were both so content in our strange little world that I didn't think anything had the power to flip this thing on its head.

Until Lydia.

One afternoon, while Richard was at work, I was messing around on his computer, surfing the web. Again, for anyone too young, surfing the web is what the Internet was used for before meme sharing, selfie posting and tweet stealing became everyday business. I had clicked to save a funny image that I wanted to email to him, but when I tried to find it in his photo file, I came across semi-naked photos of his ex-girlfriend, Lydia. I was annoyed, I guess. But not upset. It seemed fair to assume he hadn't gotten around to deleting them.

When we sat down to dinner that night, I casually mentioned the incident. He seemed sincerely apologetic that he hadn't erased the images and agreed to take care of it. That was that. I let it go.

Richard and Lydia had adopted a dog during the tenure of their relationship. However, she hadn't asked to see the pet during the first three months I was living with him. Until Lydia found out that I was, in fact, living with him.

My introduction to her was about as comfortable as accidentally seeing your dad naked. Early one morning I woke up to a woman's screams accompanied by a loud banging at the front door. I shook Richard to wake him as the noise persisted. "Who the fuck is that?" I asked him, irritated.

He hesitated as he sat up, listening to the screams. "I think it's my ex." His voice sank as he continued, "I didn't want to make a thing of it, but she found out about us a week ago and she's been acting a little nuts since."

"You should go deal with her. It's eight AM and the shop will be opening soon," I said.

You always want to seem like the superior, well-tempered vagina in a situation like this. Because A) it's pretty easy to seize that opportunity when you're not the one flailing at your ex-boyfriend's door and B) your man needs a calm voice of reason at a time like this. But let's be honest, it's mostly A. Staying on top is an art.

Richard sprung out of bed and pulled on a pair of worn-out jeans. He grabbed a t-shirt from the drawer and slipped it over his head as he ran down the stairs. He stopped before he turned the corner in the stairwell and looked back at me, "Please stay here. If she sees you, it will only make it worse."

"Oh, trust me, I have no intention of going anywhere near that," I replied.

He smiled with relief and disappeared around the corner, descending the final flight.

The kitchen window was ajar and I could hear her screams echo through the apartment. I curiously snuck closer to the window to get a better listen. The front door was directly below so I could hear everything.

"I want the fucking dog, Rich," she screamed.

"Calm down, you're not taking my dog," he responded.

"I don't want her around him," she continued to scream. As if I were some weird dog molester.

"Go home, Lydia. This is insane," he pleaded.

"Is she here?" she asked. There was a pause. "Is that bitch fucking here?" she asked again, only this time it had that charming psychotic ring to it.

"Yes, she's here. She lives here. And it's none of your business," he responded.

"Tell her to get down here. I want to talk to her," she blasted.

I could hear him nervously laugh. "We're going to leave Jordan out of this." I think the sound of my name must have flipped a switch because there was a tense pause before I heard a loud THUD. Followed by excessive banging. "Stop hitting my car," Richard yelled. The banging stopped and a silence fell between the two of them. "Go home psycho," he said before I heard the front door open and close again.

I raced back into the bedroom as he ascended the stairs. She continued to pound on the door.

"Is she going to sit there doing that all day?" I asked him.

"Probably for another ten minutes until she has to go to work. I'm sorry about this. Just ignore her."

"That's like telling me to ignore an air raid," I said over the pounding and screaming. There was one final kick to the front door before the noise suddenly stopped.

Richard and I stepped into the kitchen and peered out the window as she got back into her car. "What a maniac," he mumbled as she squealed out of the driveway.

I watched him as he watched her drive away. I was concerned. I felt an overwhelming feeling of sickness. I knew this wasn't the end of Lydia. She was going to be back. The question was whether or not I was willing to put up a fight.

* * *

A few days had passed since our encounter with Lydia. Richard started working on a new show, so I was alone at home during the days I wasn't working. One afternoon, I was sitting at the computer, composing an email to a friend who was traveling, when a loud DING blared from the speaker. I looked up at the email notification. Lydia's name taunted me from the corner of the large computer screen. I couldn't resist. Curiosity (crazy) got the best of me. I felt it was my business at this point (this in no way means it was actually my business). I clicked on the notification and the email widened over the large screen.

It was basically a long-winded rant about how horrible he was. She claimed she thought they were going to work things out. She called me a bunch of names, "butterface" being one. That was cute. Especially since we'd never been in the same room together. This was a woman so plagued with jealousy and contempt that I felt sorry for her. I read on. She began listing all the things she wanted back in her possession. Things she had paid for, from the red Impala to an Ikea shoe rack. She was like the little silver ball in a pinball machine, bouncing between anger and pettiness down the slow decline. I closed the email and marked it as unread.

I didn't mention it to Richard. I didn't want him to know I'd read his email. We had a rapport to withhold. I'd never done anything like that before. I knew it was an invasion of privacy. I should have known the second I felt the urge to read his email that it was time to get out.

Ladies, if you are ever in a position where you can't trust someone enough to give him privacy, that is a little, burrowing wood-bug called 'intuition' and it's time to pack your bags and vacate the premises. Checking someone's emails or text messages is a completely fucking crazy thing to do. Take the sane, mature approach: put on a wig and follow him around for a week. Gentlemen, if you're ever in the position where you feel the urge to go through your girlfriend's phone, you're probably dating a girl with a sponsor.

Jokes aside, women can be awful too, oftentimes worse than men. If a man cheats, it's usually for sexual completion. When women do it, it's for about four billion other reasons. But sexual completion is probably on the laundry list. In my experience, adult women cheat because they're afraid to break up and start over. When adult men cheat, it's because they probably can't afford to break up and start over.

But back to being immature non-adults.

I justified my actions by feeling that it was my right to be aware of everything that was going on, that his business was my business.

Women do this. It's this bizarre, I've been wronged once and it's my job to make sure I am not wronged twice, mentality. But it's just an excuse. If you can't trust a man, walk away. Nine times out of ten that intuitive wood-bug is correct.

As the obvious descent of my sanity would have it, Richard slowly drifted away. He began talking to Lydia again. He claimed it was just friendly, that he had to make nice with her or she would take the dog. He said it had to be this way to keep the peace. I just couldn't understand why and I was sick of living in his sad-bastard country song. So, I did what any stable person would do, I tapped into his email again. Confessions of a drunk writer.

Crazy Level: 7.1 The first time you invade someone's privacy, you get a mulligan. I'd rate a first-time offender at about a 5.2. But once you become a repeat offender, you've left cruise control.

I opened the most recent email from Lydia and there was a string of back-and-forth correspondences between the two of them. Once I dug deep enough into the thread, I learned that Richard and I were breaking up and that I was moving out. He made it sound like I was some young, pathetic vagabond with nowhere to go. As though he was doing a public service by letting me stay there while I sorted out some existential crisis. I was appalled and grossed out. So I grabbed my poetry journal and took my existential crisis to the pub up the street.

I sat there for hours, writing down all my rhyming emo thoughts. For any young poets out there, here's a tip: poetry doesn't actually solve anything and it probably won't change your life. Take it from me, a 31-year-old struggling writer, stay in school.

By the time I decided to pack it in, I realized he'd probably been home for hours and I'd left my cellphone at the apartment in my fit of frustration. Remember what that was like? When you could do things without living in constant terror of missing out on what's going on everywhere else. Nowadays, people would sooner forget their child in the car than their cellphone.

I decided to walk home. I knew I had to confront him. I couldn't go through what I went through with Billy again. I didn't have it in me. I needed to find my backbone and assert some dominance in this situation, before it trampled all over me. I went over the conversation in my head a million times before I reached the alternator shop. I stuck my key in the lock and took a deep breath before opening the door. I made my way up the stairs to find him in the living room with Steve.

"Where have you been?" he asked.

"Writing."

"Oh. We were worried. We ordered pizza because we assumed you weren't cooking dinner tonight," he stated in a passive-aggressive tone.

"Cool." I said as I walked into the bedroom. He got up and followed me.

"What's going on?" he asked.

"I don't know. You tell me," I paused for a moment to consider what I was about to say and then the words just fell out of my mouth, "You're the one with the hidden agenda!"

"What's that supposed to mean?" he asked.

I thought about beating around the bush, using reverse psychology, but quickly decided against it because I didn't have enough time to concoct any bullshit. Instead, I straightened my spine and just came out with it, guns blazing. "What's going on with Lydia? Do you want me to move out?"

"Where is this coming from?" he asked.

"Something isn't right and I want to know what it is," I demanded.

"You're acting hysterical. Nothing is wrong. What's this about?" he probed.

"Don't fucking lie to me. I saw the email," I blurted.

"What email? Why are you going through my emails?" he started to panic.

I grinded my teeth at his dismissive reversal, "You know exactly what I'm talking about. Why are you telling her we're breaking up and that I'm moving out?"

"I'm just trying to make her go away. Jesus Christ. She's asking me for a ton of money for the stuff we bought together and it's the only way I can get her off my back. If she thinks you're out of the picture, she will stop giving a shit about any of it. Why the fuck are you reading my emails?"

I stared at him. Why was I going through his emails? "I've been in this situation before. You're being secretive and I wanted answers," I replied.

"You aren't this person. Stop acting crazy. I don't need two whackos in my life right now. One is enough. You're better than this," he said, quickly turning it around.

I immediately felt guilty and pushed my feelings to the wayside. What the hell was wrong with me? He was right. I was turning into a crazy person. "I'm sorry," I said as I recoiled back into the fetal position.

He looked at me forgivingly. "Okay, can we get back to our original program here? I hope you like Hawaiian." Richard had a way with manipulation. He didn't explain why he had to lie about me to get her off his back. And I didn't ask. You would think I would have known better by this point not to put up with this type of evasive behavior, but clearly, I was suffering from emotional dementia.

* * *

Things started to go back to normal. Lydia eventually left us alone and the drama subsided. We spent the holidays on the island splitting our time between family and friends. I spent a few nights at his parents' home in the woods, where we drank whiskey and the boys played guitar around the kitchen table. I hadn't had that much fun during the holiday season since I was a kid. Richard's family was spirited, kind and grounded. Everyone was always welcome there. I could probably show up on their doorstep tomorrow with a suitcase, two dogs, a parakeet and a heroin addiction and they'd offer me a place to live.

After the New Year, we got back to the city. Richard had to work and I had to get back to, well, all the arbitrary day to day shit I wasted my time doing, like writing poetry. I had actually begun writing a memoir at the time, I guess I felt my inexperience was exactly the type of thing people would be interested in reading about (insert exaggerated eye roll here). I gave up on it after about 150 hand-written pages when I realized how narcissistic the memoir of a delusional 19-year-old would be. People often ask if I'll ever pick it up again to finish it. The answer is no. Trying to sound serious about simultaneously battling eating disorders and puberty is about as original as throwing a white party.

One cold, January morning, I woke up to a loud SMACK. As I came to consciousness, I saw a woman's backside exit the bedroom as she slammed the bedroom door and ran down the stairs. I looked at Richard, who was paralyzed from shock. His left cheek turned bright red. He sat up confused. "What the fuck just happened?" he asked.

"I think Lydia just happened," I said coldly.

He quickly sprung out of bed, threw on some old dregs and flew down the stairs. I heard the front door open and then slam shut.

I could hear them yelling back and forth, unable to really make out the conversation. Finally, I heard tires peel out of the driveway and the front door open and close again. He came upstairs to find me sitting on the couch in the living room, practically naked, staring at the black TV screen.

"Are you okay?" he asked.

"Would you be?" I responded.

"I'm really sorry, Steve must have forgot to lock the door this morning on his way to work," he started, "I don't know what she's thinking."

"I don't really care," I said, "you told me this had been dealt with. Clearly it hasn't. Your past isn't supposed to be my problem."

"I have no idea why she's doing this. Someone told her you were at my parents' place this Christmas and I guess it's pushed her over the edge," he said.

"Why are you making excuses for her behavior?" I threw back.

"She's just hurt that I've moved on," he said, again making excuses for her.

"Let's go back for a minute here. This is someone who showed up at your place at 8 AM, came in through the front door, walked into your bedroom and slapped you in the face while we were dead asleep. All because she's upset that I spent time with you over the holidays? That is the behavior of someone who needs to be medicated."

"What do you want me to do? Tell her to fuck off? You know I can't do that." His blood was starting to boil.

"Yes! That's exactly what you should do. Tell her to go the fuck away because she's toxic. How is this a concept that I have to explain to a 30-year-old man?" I fired.

"Stop it. You know that's cruel. I can't do that." He looked to the window.

Asshole Rating: 6 While this one doesn't feel like it should land on the Asshole Scale because it's technically the opposite of being an asshole, he was only choosing to spare her feelings so that he could save a few bucks.

"Why, because she owns you? Because you don't want to part with the computer she bought? Or any of the other material garbage? Give me a break. This is insane and I can't believe I'm sitting here having this conversation. I need a drink," I said, exhausted.

"It's eight thirty in the morning. You don't need a drink. Let's go for breakfast," he said trying to calm me down.

"No thanks. I need to get out of this house for a while. Alone. You can call your poor ex-girlfriend and console her. I'm taking the day off from this zoo," I said as I got up, making my way to the bathroom.

I came back to the apartment later that night to find Richard in the bedroom, playing guitar. He stopped when I walked in and looked over to me. There was a long pause before he finally broke the silence, "Are we going to be alright?" he asked.

"I don't honestly know. But Ally's on her way over to pick me up. I'm going to spend a few days at her place to figure out what I'm doing here. I'm not happy anymore. I can't play second fiddle to your ex. So, if being with me is something that's important to you, I suggest you sort out your feelings," I responded.

Ally and I stayed up all night drinking wine and talking about our relationships. It was exactly what I needed. Around midnight my cell-phone buzzed. It was Richard. I decided not to answer it. We were having a good time and I didn't want to dampen that.

He called back a couple hours later as I was starting to fall asleep on the couch. Ally had gone to bed so I answered it. "Hello?"

"Hey. What are you doing?" he asked eagerly.

"It's almost three in the morning, I'm going to sleep," I said slightly irritated.

"Did you go out tonight?" he asked.

"No, we picked up a few bottles of wine and hung out at the house," I said, growing more irritated.

"Oh. That sounds nice." He trailed off.

"Rich, why are you calling?" I finally cut to it.

Pause.

"I wanted to tell you I'm sorry. You're right. You shouldn't have to deal with this shit. It's not fair," he said.

I sat in silence. I wasn't expecting an apology.

"Please come home," he blurted.

"When you tell Lydia to piss off. Until then I don't want to be around you."

"I already have. I had a long conversation with her this afternoon. I told her I was with you now and that she had to stop the nonsense. She won't be bothering us anymore," he assured.

"Really?"

"Yes, really. You have my word. So please come home tomorrow. I can pick you up around noon."

I thought about it for a minute. "Okay," I finally agreed.

"Okay, get to sleep, night owl."

"You too." I hung up.

* * *

Things returned to normal over the following month. The night before Valentine's Day, Richard and his roommate invited a few friends over for a poker game. I'd become friends with Nicole, a sweet blonde girl who was dating Richard's friend. She decided to come over and keep me company while the boys gambled. The two of us hung out in the living room and drank wine for the majority of the night. Nicole and Lydia were friends, so I was always careful to keep our conversation relatively surface-level. I didn't want to invite any unwanted drama.

Once the boys were finished, they joined us in the living room. Richard sat down next to me, resting his hand on my leg.

The group was laughing and sharing stories when Richard's phone lit up on the end table. I looked over as the phone silently rang. I recognized the number on the screen right away. Lydia. I ignored it. Then it rang again. I ignored it again. But it continued to ring. Finally, I leaned toward Richard and whispered, "Lydia is calling. It's the fifth time she's called."

He tensed up. He leaned over me, reaching for his phone. It was still ringing. He let it be. The screen went dark. We both watched it for a few seconds, waiting. And then it lit up again. This was the seventh time she'd called in a row. Neither of us wanted to make a scene in front of everyone, but it was too late. I looked up and noticed the group had fallen silent as everyone eyed the phone uncomfortably like it was the trailer park aunt who gets too drunk at your wedding and awkwardly flashes all the guests during the Chicken Dance.

Richard stood up. "Sorry guys, I just have to take this," he said as he excused himself from the living room. He stepped into his bedroom and closed the door. Nicole tossed a scornful look in my direction. She knew who it was. I threw back an affirmative eye roll in response.

She got up and made her way to the couch and sat next to me while the boys carried on. "Lydia again?" she whispered.

"How did you guess?" I said sarcastically.

"I don't know how you put up with this. I mean she's my friend, but she's completely lost her mind over you."

"It's not really my business, but what happened between them? Why did they break up?" I asked quietly.

"He's never told you?" she seemed genuinely shocked. I shook my head and she continued, "Lydia slept with one of his friends while they were on a break. He was pretty busted up over it and refused to take her back."

"Well why the fuck does he even entertain her shit then? I don't get it," I said.

"Lydia had the money in their relationship. The car is technically hers, the computer, his phone is in her name, everything. He owes her money for all this shit if he wants her to disappear. Until then she can lord it all over him. At the end of the day, she's jealous. He's moved on and she hasn't," she said as Richard appeared. Nicole smiled then got up to make room for him. He sat down.

"I'm sorry about that. She's lost her mind," he said quietly to me. "I told her to fuck off."

I looked at him with obvious disbelief. He was lying.

That night I lay awake, staring at the ceiling. Richard was passed out next to me as my mind ran wild. I wanted to know what was said on the phone. Why she was calling. I wanted to know what he wasn't telling me. I turned onto my side in an attempt to fall sleep. I was about to close my eyes, when I saw something flash across the room. I focused on the computer desk. His phone had lit up. I watched the flash for a few moments before curiosity engulfed me. I slowly sat up in bed. Before making another move, I looked back to see if Richard stirred. He was out cold. I stealthily got out of the bed and tiptoed across the bedroom. I sat down in the desk chair and picked up his phone. I looked over at the bed. He was still asleep. I stared at his phone for a minute while the devil and the angel perched on opposing shoulders squabbled back and forth until finally, I flipped it open. There were three missed calls and two voicemails. I clicked on the voicemail notification and moved the receiver to my ear as it dialed his mailbox. An automated voice loudly came over the receiver. It startled me as I fumbled to turn down the volume. I quickly glanced over to the bed to make sure Richard was still asleep. He hadn't moved.

I put the phone back to my ear as the automated voice asked for the password. Shit. I thought for a minute and typed in '1973'. The automated voice told me that was incorrect and to try again. I thought for a moment and typed in the numbers that spelled 'RICH'. Wrong again. A feeling of defeat blew through me as I realized that this could take all night. It really doesn't take much to defeat you when you're 20. I sat up and decided to give it one more shot before calling it quits. I typed in 'oooo' and then waited anxiously for the automated voice. "You have two unheard voice messages. Press ONE to hear your messages." Got it! I pressed one. "First NEW message."

The voicemail began with heavy breathing, then, "Richard, please stop ignoring my calls. Please," a sobbing voice started in. "I can't live without you. I don't want to live without you. Please stop ignoring my calls. This isn't fair. I thought you were breaking up with her. She's still there. I know she's there. You promised you were kicking her out for good." Lydia's crackling nasal cry-voice pleaded over the speaker. I snapped the phone closed and set it back on the desk. I'd heard enough. I sat in the chair staring at the black computer screen. Finally, I got up and crawled back into bed.

I woke up the next morning to the sound of Lydia's adenoidal sobbing in my head. I looked over at Richard while he slept. I looked at my phone. February 14th. Great. *"Well,"* I thought to myself, *"what better day for a breakup than Valentine's Day?"*

I got up to shower.

When I toweled off and entered the bedroom, Richard was up, sitting in front of his computer. I was draped in a robe with a towel wrapped around my hair. I sat on the bed as I spun the towel away from my head and began drying my hair with it. He watched me curiously. Neither of us said a word. I walked over to my over-flowing suitcase and picked out something to wear. I quickly got dressed in silence. He knew something was wrong but he didn't want to address it. I pulled all of my clothing out of the suitcase and passive-aggressively began neatly folding everything back into it.

As I finished, Richard finally spoke. "What's up?"

I ignored him as I got up from the floor and grabbed my journal off the shelf. I threw it on top of my clothes, then reached down, closed the lid of my suitcase, and zipped it up.

"Uh, are you going somewhere?" he asked anxiously.

I looked at him. "Yes. I am. I'm going to Ally's house. I'm staying there for a while until I find my own place."

A look of panic contaminated his previously calm demeanor. His eyes filled with sadness. He was about to fight, but then something hit him and he chose against it. "Maybe it's for the best."

I was stunned. I guess I expected him to be upset, or make excuses, something. But he was defeated too. We just looked at each other in silence.

I heard a honk from outside. Ally. I shook my head at him, disappointed. I picked up the heavy suitcase and struggled to get it to the bedroom door. Richard stood up and swept the oversized luggage from my grasp. He carried the bulky, cumbersome suitcase down the stairs as I followed behind. He loaded the bag into Ally's backseat as I climbed into the passenger side and closed the door. I stared out the window at Richard as we started to roll past him. He mouthed "I love you," before fading out of sight.

* * *

A few weeks later I learned that Richard was moving in with Lydia. This was hardly surprising, as I always knew he was a kept man. He wasn't capable of independence because he'd dug himself into such a massive financial hole that he needed support to stay afloat. However, I won't say I wasn't heartbroken. I always hoped he was stronger than that. One thing I've definitely learned in love is that too often your hopes go astray.

Richard contacted me through email not too long after he'd moved in with Lydia. It was a longwinded apology. At the end of the email, he asked if I would meet him for coffee or dinner. I didn't respond right away. It took me a little while to compose a reply. If there was anything I'd learned from my experience, it's that there was a game being played here. I had to proceed with caution.

My email response was wordy and nothing short of cruel. I intended to make Richard understand how hurt I was without sounding pathetic or weak. Once I finished, I read it over about 20 times before I finally clicked send. I sat back in the rolling chair, clasping my hands on the desk in front of the computer, as I smiled with satisfaction. I knew he would get it that night. I knew he wouldn't respond until the following day. And I knew I had ruined all those hours in between for him. It felt good. Which I understand is slightly psychosomatic. But when someone breaks your heart, there's a part of your twisted brain that possesses a thirst for their suffering. The human race is a malicious infection on an otherwise pleasant planet. We're all going to Hell in a cheaply manufactured hand basket.

Richard's reply came right on time the following morning. I couldn't open the email fast enough. It felt like Christmas. His response was short and poignant. He claimed he hadn't realized how much he had hurt me and that my email was hard to swallow. Before signing off he asked if we could meet up so that he could properly apologize. He didn't feel good with how things were left and he felt I deserved more. This was precisely how I anticipated things would go. I responded to say it wasn't necessary but if he felt it was important, I would make time. His second reply was almost immediate and he said he would pick me up the following day around three.

He showed up 15 minutes early that wet Tuesday afternoon. Winter was over and spring was making its seasonal entry which, in Vancouver, means it's still just raining. He called when he was out front. I ran from the door to the car with my jacket hauled over my head to avoid getting my hair wet. As I approached the car he got out and ran around to open the passenger door. This type of chivalry was completely out of his character. Richard was neglectful and not exactly perceptive. He was making an effort. I jumped in and he closed the door behind me. He ran around the back and hopped into the driver's seat. He let out a dramatic "Brrr" and turned towards me. "Thank you for making time to see me."

This was feeling contrived. What the hell was happening here? Opening doors and thanking me for my time? This was not the Richard that I was used to.

We decided on a little Italian restaurant he was familiar with in Ally's neighborhood. When we sat down at our table, he asked questions about how I was doing, what I had been up to, essentially just making small talk until we finally placed our order with the waiter. It was borderline painful and I regretted showering and changing out of my sweatpants for this.

"So what's up?" I asked. "Why are we here right now?"

He hesitated, "I wanted to apologize to you. I know I hurt you and you didn't deserve that."

"I see," I responded. "You seriously just invited me to dinner to apologize? This has to be about something else."

"It's not. I worry about you. I wanted to make sure you were okay, that we were okay," he replied.

I sat there staring at him coldly. I don't know what I wanted. I guess I assumed he was here to tell me what a huge mistake he'd made moving in with her. That he missed me. That they were breaking up and he wanted to give us another shot. That he loved me. That Lydia had been swallowed by a whale after a freak boating accident and we were finally free from her financial claws. Anything. Not just "I'm sorry".

"Does she know you're here?" I finally asked him.

"Well, no, not exactly. I mean…"

I cut him off. "So you're running around behind her back to tell me you're sorry? Why? Do you feel better now? Do you feel right with all the shit you've put everyone through?" I snapped.

"Jordan, this is a really tough spot for me. Lydia loves me. She would do anything for me." He was starting to realize this was a mistake. "You don't understand. You're young. You have a life ahead of you. One I don't want to keep you from. You stick with me and you'll end up like me. Trust me, you don't want that."

Tears began to well. I tried to hold them back as the waiter brought our food to the table. I looked away as Richard thanked him.

"All you keep saying is Lydia loves me but you've never once said that you love her. Do you?" I stared at him.

He looked up at me and then down at his plate. Finally, he responded, "I guess I do, yeah."

"You guess you do? You're living with this person and you only guess you love her?" I said raising my voice again.

He was starting to grow agitated. "I don't know exactly what I feel for her right now. We're working it out. Do I love her? Sure, I love her like I love my friends and my dog, am I in love with her? No, I'm not. If you want the truth, I love you. I'm in love with you. But the future looks good with Lydia." He stopped himself, realizing what he had just said. He looked down as he grabbed a forkful of spaghetti. "Is that what you wanted to hear?"

Asshole Rating: 7.5 Because who fucking says that?

Tears rolled down my cheeks as I plucked a forkful of pasta from my dish and attempted to chew it. I'd lost my appetite. "I'm ready to get the bill," I said as I got up and excused myself to the restroom. The drive home was uncomfortably silent. He pulled up to Ally's house and I opened the door to get out. He grabbed my arm.

"Richard, please." I glared at him.

"I don't want you to be upset. That wasn't the point of this," he said as I closed the car door to avoid getting wet.

"Okay, well enlighten me then, what was the point of this? From where I'm standing, it looks like some jerk's desperate attempt for the last word," I huffed. "We already broke up, remember? No need to relive that."

"I don't want you to get out of this car and hate me," he begged. "I want us to be friends. I don't want to lose you. I want to know there's still a chance somewhere down the road."

"What the fuck is that? You can't just keep me on some backburner while you two play house in whatever asylum you've built together," I said, irritated.

"That's not what I mean. Listen, can we please try to leave this conversation amicably?" he pleaded. I swung the passenger door open and escorted myself out of the car. I slammed the door behind me and began to storm off. He rolled down the window. "Jordan, please don't," he called after me.

I stopped and spun around. "I'm just finishing what you started. And then finished. And then started again," I yelled back. I turned around and marched toward the house as the rain soaked my face, disguising my tears.

* * *

About two months later I moved into my own place and locked down a job at a local retail store. I received a text from Richard one night while I was up writing. He was in Ally's neighborhood and wanted to meet for a drink. Every instinct I had told me to ignore the text. But I couldn't. He still had a hold on me. I responded telling him I'd moved.

A few seconds later, my phone rang. I watched his number blink on my call display before finally answering. "What's up?" I said.

"Where did you move to?" he asked.

"What's it to you?" I fired at him.

"Humor me," he responded.

"Corner of Sixteenth and Burrard," I answered.

"Luckily for you I'm only twenty minutes away from there. You should probably pull yourself together," he joked just before hanging up. He didn't give me an opportunity to decline. Because that's totally what I would have done, being 20 and desperate for attention and all.

I pulled myself together and in just under 30 minutes, his lights flashed through the living room window from outside. I opened my front door and heard The Cramps blaring from his old BMW. I turned to lock up.

His window was rolled down as I approached the vehicle. "Stalking people is illegal. You know that, right?" I said with a smile on my face.

"Yeah, yeah," he said as I made my way to passenger side. I opened the door and once again sat my ass where it didn't belong.

"Where to?" I asked as he peeled out.

"I have a bottle of wine and the means to escape. Anywhere but this life would be a good start," he laughed as we pulled out.

I knew we were heading to the beach. I rested my head against the seat and closed my eyes. The wind blew through my hair, causing it to whip against my face, like the ice-cold slap of reality. That I ignored.

Richard parked in the secluded brush at Spanish Banks. He reached into the back seat to grab the bottle of wine. I laughed as he showed me the label. "What?" he said with a smile.

"Cheap shiraz still, huh?" I heckled him as he twisted the cap off.

"Oh, I'm sorry. Next time I'll be sure to spend forty dollars on a bottle of wine I'll probably hate," he replied only half joking. He passed me the bottle and I took a long sip.

We spent an hour talking. Well, I spent an hour talking. He spent the hour cracking jokes and avoiding any mention of Lydia.

As I took the last sip of wine from the bottle I looked at him, half-drunk, "I think we need more wine."

He paused, looking at me for a long moment with his head cocked against his seat. "I think I really miss you," he said as he leaned towards my lips.

I pulled away. "Whoa." I drunkenly shook my head. "Don't you have a girlfriend that you live with?"

"I really didn't want to talk about it, but I doubt I'll be living there much longer," he responded. That should not have been enough for me. But I wanted it to be enough. So, I let it be. He leaned in again, and this time I let him. We kissed for a while before he slowly leaned back into his seat and started the car.

"Where are we going?" I asked.

"Probably to Hell. But before that we're going to your place," he laughed.

We parked in the back alley and he followed me inside. "Excuse the mess," I said to him as we walked through the door. "I'm still unpacking."

"That's cool. Where's your room?" he asked, poking his head around. I pointed to the door on the other side of the living room of the small basement suite. He surged into my room and flopped down on my bed. I followed behind, stopping in the doorway. "Got any wine?" he asked as he made himself comfortable and flipped on the stereo.

"I think so," I replied as I turned and made my way into the kitchen. The bottle I'd picked up earlier that night was sitting on the counter. I held it up to the light to see what was left of it. "Enough for a nightcap," I yelled toward the bedroom. I poured two large glasses and went back to the room.

"Decent place," he said as he looked around, scanning the books on the floor.

"It's okay. I'm just glad to be in my own space again." I handed him a glass of wine as he shot an offensive look. "Not that I didn't like living with you guys." I tried to save it. "But you know what I mean," I said and then gave up.

He pulled me toward him. I resisted his grasp as I tossed back the entire glass of wine in one smooth gulp. My final act of restraint before we dove into each other.

I woke up around 4 AM to the sound of tires peeling through the gravel in the back alley. I groggily looked around, realizing Richard had left. My hangover was starting to set in. I got out of bed naked and stumbled to the kitchen. I opened the fridge door to find a half-empty jar of blueberry jam, old spaghetti leftovers, expired milk, and a Budweiser. I shrugged as I reached for the beer, popped the cap and lifted the bottle to my lips in desperate hopes that it would consume my hangover and my regret.

I woke up the next morning to a text message from Richard. *"Had a lot of fun with you last night. I'll call you this week."* I decided not to respond. I was happy to carry on with my week avoiding whatever floodgate I'd opened. Not my finest hour.

* * *

Over the course of the following month, Richard continued to show up, usually unannounced. We would go to quiet bars where no one recognized us. We would drink, laugh and listen to music before winding up back at my place between the sheets. He always arrived with gifts, and by "gifts" I mean sex toys and alcohol. I was basically his escort. I say escort because hooker always sounds like someone with scabs and a meth-induced under bite. So, I was a cheap and somewhat tasteless escort, with unconventionally low, albeit hilarious standards.

He stuck to the story that they were broken up, but that they were sorting through the damage of the relationship. I knew better. I'd heard this story before. I knew what was going on and where it was going to end up. I wasn't stupid. I just chose to act stupid. I loved the guy. And I hated Lydia. Call me a cunt. I certainly acted like one. Call me whatever you like, but I wanted her to suffer for trampling all over my contently autonomous relationship.

Crazy Level: 7.5 Contrary to popular belief, it is crazy to put your own selfish bullshit ahead of someone else's pain, whether you feel they deserve it or not.

Sound familiar? This is what happens when you're incapable of controlling your inner crazy. You become a horrible, wretched bottom-feeder. You start recreating the horrors of your past because you're so bitter and self-destructive that you forget to remind yourself of what it felt like at the bottom. So you fester in your pit until all that shitty karma comes crashing over you. Which it did, oh how it did.

* * *

When my period hadn't showed up in seven weeks, I began to panic. After a few days listening to my neurosis, Ally showed with a pregnancy test. I think I'd hoped that if I just avoided dealing with it, it would go away. However, similar to filing your taxes, that's never the case.

The following morning, I peed on the stick like the package instructed. I set the uterus thermometer on the bathroom counter and tried to distract myself while I awaited my impending doom. I paced around my living room, flicking the TV on... and then off. I opened and closed the fridge door about nine times looking for a bite to eat, hoping the blueberry jam would morph into a slice of pizza. I looked at the clock. It was the longest three minutes of my life, but they had finally passed. My heart rate sped up as I made my way into the bathroom. I looked at the counter from the entrance as the white stick gleamed under the vanity lights. I took a deep breath and reached for the life-ruiner. I closed my eyes, begging for a negative result. I opened my eyes. To my horror, a blue plus sign beamed up at me. It was taunting me and I was terrified. My life was over. I'd completely fucked it all up. I was going to have to quit my job folding sweaters for minimum wage and move into a trailer park. It would be Kraft Dinner and Wonder Bread from here on out. All my dreams came crashing down around me like a Jonestown Kool-Aid party. No more vacations, no more silence, no more sleep and no more binge drinking myself to near death. My life, as I knew it, was about to end and everything moving forward would smell like baby powder and diarrhea. Fuck.

The room started to blur and dizziness set in. I sat down on the toilet.

An hour passed before I finally got up to find my phone. I called Ally.

I spent the following few days dodging Richard's calls. I didn't really know how to tell him. I also didn't really know if I wanted to. I wasn't ready to be a parent. He definitely wasn't ready to be a parent. He wasn't even ready to part with a shoe rack and pay his own phone bill.

I eventually received an urgent message from him, claiming we needed to talk. I thought maybe Ally told him about the pregnancy test. I responded saying I was available that night.

There was a knock at my front entrance around 8 o'clock. I opened the door to a disheveled man. Richard looked like he hadn't slept in days. He was distraught and antsy. *"He knows,"* I thought. "Listen," I said as he walked through the front door, "I only didn't tell you because I wasn't sure how or if I was ready. I still don't really know what I'm going to do."

"Huh? What are you talking about?" he asked.

"I thought that's what you wanted to talk about?" I replied.

"Okay, what? What did you think I wanted to talk about?" He was more confused than I was.

"The pregnancy test," I responded.

He stared at me blankly before he fell back onto the loveseat propped perfectly behind him, "You're fucking pregnant?"

"Okay, you need to explain what's going on here?" I continued, "And I only think I'm pregnant. I took a pregnancy test but they can be unreliable. I still have to see a doctor."

"Fuck." He said. "Fuck, fuck, fuck."

"What's going on? Why did you need to talk to me then?" I asked.

He froze. I stared at him waiting for an answer. "I'm just going to say it," he took a breath, "Lydia bought a house in Hope. She's asked me to move there with her to start fresh."

Hope. How fucking apropos.

Fury burrowed inside of me. He could see it. His eyes filled with fear as he watched me turn into the Hulk. I snapped my head back and then slowly brought it forward as I channeled Regan MacNeil. We both stood in silence and my eyes burst out of their sockets. Then, like the howling of a hurricane breaching in the distance, I exhaled before the rush of destruction. I tore up one side of him and down the other. I can't even remember what I said. Everything became a specific shade of bright red. I screamed at him to leave. I wanted him out. He finally backed toward the entrance and as he stepped through it, I slammed the door in his face.

I stood there until I heard his car drive away. When the music disappeared, the anger went with it. Suddenly aware of where I was and what had just happened. I broke into sobs as I fell to the floor. How did I wind up here? I could feel every muscle in my heart snap as my stomach burned into knots. My whole body was on fire. I laid on my living room floor for hours. Staring at the ceiling. Music played in the background as everything began to fall apart. Cracks tore through the popcorn ceiling, shedding chunks of paint and the walls peeled and crumbled around me in a haze of emotional erosion. Everything began to fade to black.

I woke up to the sound of my phone ringing. I looked at the clock on the wall. 11:11 PM. "*Go figure*," I thought to myself as I rolled my eyes and made a wish that I wasn't pregnant. I reached for my phone on the coffee table. Ally's name flashed on the LCD screen. I couldn't bring myself to answer. I sat up and shook myself awake as I let the phone ring. The anger flooded back. I decided I had to call Richard.

I dialed his number. It rang about four times before the voicemail picked up. I hung up. I waited 15 minutes and decided to call again. It rang once before a girl's voice answered, "Hello?"

"Uh hi. I'm looking for Richard, is he around?" I asked. I knew exactly who was on the other end.

"He's busy. What do you want?" Lydia snapped. I could feel her homicidal rage begin to rise.

"I really need to talk to Rich, Lydia. Just put him on the phone," I said annoyed with her dominant tone.

"I said he's busy. Besides, anything you have to say to him, you can say to me," she erupted.

I rolled my neck back with agitation, realizing he was probably sitting right next to her, I decided in that moment to just out the bastard,

"Okay, fine," I paused as my nerves gyrated through every muscle in my body, "I might be pregnant."

Silence. Then, click. She'd hung up on me.

Two minutes later, my phone rang. "Hello?" I answered in an annoyed tone, expecting to hear Richard's voice.

Lydia's voice blasted over the speaker, "Jordan, women have been getting abortions for years. Just deal with it." Then, click.

My phone rang the next morning. It was Richard. I decided to answer it.

"What?"

"We need to see a doctor," he sounded concerned but I knew better.

"I've made an appointment for Thursday afternoon. You can come or not. I don't care," I said annoyed.

"I'll be there," he responded. The line went quiet. "I'm really sorry about what happened last night. She's gone off the rails. I promise whatever happens here, we'll get through it together," he said.

There was a long pause. "I'll see you Thursday," I finally responded before abruptly hanging up the phone.

That night I cried.

* * *

It was 3:30 on Thursday when Richard picked me up. As he pulled into a parking space outside the clinic, he asked if I wanted him to come in. I didn't really want him in there. If it turned out I was pregnant, I had no idea what kind of physical reaction I might have. I said no and told him he could wait in the car.

I made my way inside where I was greeted by a receptionist and after a short wait, I was escorted to a private examination room.

"Miss West, what can I help you with today?" the doctor asked, looking at his clipboard as he entered the room.

"Well," I started nervously. "My period is about two months late. I took a pregnancy test a week ago and it read positive. I'm hoping you can tell me the test was wrong."

"Hmm," he said as he curiously looked up at me. "Are your periods usually abnormal?" he asked.

"Sometimes," I said.

He reached into the cupboard and handed me a jar. "We'll run another test. I just need a urine sample."

I sat on the cold examination table after handing off my pee to the stranger and looked around the room as I waited for him to return. A few minutes later, the door opened and the doctor appeared. He eyed me curiously. "Good news. You're not pregnant. Looks like you just bought a faulty test. Happens all the time." A wave of relief passed through me. He continued with more medical jargon about birth control but I was too busy thinking about all the life I hadn't been robbed of to pay any attention.

I thanked the doctor for his time and hopped off the table. I skipped past the receptionist and she called after me to make another appointment. I ignored her as I exited the building into the cool summer night air.

Richard was waiting for me in the parking lot. As I approached the car I stopped, remembering his words, *"we'll get through it together."* Now there was nothing to get through and like a punch to the gut, I knew it was over. Lydia was still in the picture, despite his lies. She wouldn't let him go and he wouldn't give up his situation. My eyes began to well. I opened the car door and sat down in the passenger seat.

"What's wrong?" he asked.

I didn't respond. His concern was genuine, maybe for the first time.

"Whatever it is, we can handle it. What did the doctor say? Are you pregnant?"

I started to panic. Deep down I was happy I wasn't pregnant, but I didn't want to lose him. I loved him and this felt like a chance. (Reader's note: As a rule of thumb, I don't regret any of my choices in this life. The mistakes I've made have all come with valuable lessons. However, what happened next is probably the only real regret that I've ever had to live with.)

I stared down into my lap and nodded. And then I cried. Not because I was trying to sell anything, but because I couldn't believe what I was doing. This torrid love affair had turned me into the worst possible type of person. The type of person I despised. I'd become one of those lunatics who people write psychological thrillers about; the kind where the antagonist stalks and torments some poor family, savagely murders their pet and then ultimately meets their demise when they're stabbed with a letter opener or shot in a bathtub. I had become Glenn Close in *Fatal Attraction*.

Richard took a deep breath and closed his eyes as he sunk into the driver's seat. He opened his eyes and stared into the distance. "Well what next? What do you want to do?"

"I don't know. I want to go home," I replied.

We didn't say a word to each other the entire drive home. When he pulled into the back alley, he said he would call me the next day as I stepped out the car.

Crazy Level: 9.1 This type of crazy falls right between smelling your boyfriend's penis for a hint of infidelity and cutting the brake lines in his car.

My deceit followed me around the next day like an evil monster that had its claws sunk into the flesh of my back. I didn't answer Richard's call. I skulked around my apartment all day feeling low, haunted, and sorry for myself. I knew I was fucking with the natural course of things. I knew I was causing a shift in people's lives and I knew it was wrong. Most of all, I knew I was out of my goddamn mind. I tossed and turned in bed that night, suffering from insomnia and delusion. I knew I couldn't keep up with the psycho I'd become.

Suddenly my phone rang. I turned over to look at the call display, expecting it to be Richard. It was my mother. I looked at the alarm clock on my nightstand. It was 1 AM, which meant it was 4 AM her time.

"Hello?" I answered.

"Hey kid." She sounded groggy and concerned. "Is everything okay?"

"It's late mom, I should be asking you the same thing."

"I had a really strange dream about you and felt I should check in." She paused. When I didn't respond, she continued, "You were about four and I could hear you crying but I couldn't find you. I was running around in a panic and your cries just grew more distant. Anyways, I woke up and thought I should call you. Make sure everything was okay." My mother has had intuitive dreams for as long as I can remember. When I was a kid and I was lying about something, she'd catch me by dreaming that I was lying. Her subconscious has always been on another level.

"I'm okay. I guess," I choked out.

"You don't sound okay, you sound like you've been crying," she said.

"Well," I started. "Richard and I aren't working. I did something I'm not proud of and I have no idea how to fix it."

"I thought you two broke up a long time ago. I didn't realize you were still seeing each other." I could hear the concern in her voice.

I told her the whole story. Up to the pregnancy scare. I couldn't admit to her that I thought I was pregnant and was now lying about it.

"Well, it sounds like you need to walk away. Clearly, he's invested in Lydia and as much as you dislike her, she doesn't deserve what you two are doing to her. Pull the plug. He's made his choice. Women need to start taking care of one another, it's not like there's a shortage of men in this world." She was right. I'd gotten so caught up in the competition that I forgot what I was even competing for.

"Thanks for calling, Mom. You should get back to sleep," I said.

"You too, kid. Goodnight."

We hung up. I stared at my phone for a few minutes before finally dialing Richard's number. It rang four times before he picked up, "Hello?" he sounded rushed.

"Hey. I just wanted to let you know that I'm not pregnant. It was a false alarm. So, you can continue with your life now. Take care of yourself." Without giving him an opportunity to respond, I hung up.

It was probably for the best. I had no business trying to keep a kept man. I could barely keep up with the rent.

CHAPTER 4.5:
VENGEANCE

"You can't always get what you want, but you can always get crabs."

—A quote I saw on a t-shirt once

I'M not entirely sure at what point you're supposed to stop and realize that you've crossed the line and probably belong in a straitjacket. But I suppose when you make a conscious choice to deliberately screw someone else's life up, that might be your cue. I can't take back the lie but I can promise that I've paid for it. Karma is only a bitch if you are. That was probably the biggest lesson I learned from my relationship with the Co-dependent.

When I first met him, I wasn't privy all the baggage that he was dragging behind him. I certainly wasn't expecting to encounter what came to fruition between him and Lydia. For someone to look you in the eye and tell you that they are in love with you but that their future looks better with someone else is a pretty fucking grim reality. This is someone who either lied, or actually preferred to be miserable in their relationship if it meant they could have an ATV and a heated garage. I'll never understand the world gold-diggers create for themselves. Especially when the person holding the shovel is male. Women tend to harbor less dignity than men when it comes to their finances.

* * *

Let's take a look at my favorite kept-man in recent history, Kevin Federline, or K-Fed as he was quickly dubbed, probably by Kevin himself. Now, to this moron's credit, at least he chose wisely. He found the richest, fastest downward-spiraling lunatic of 2004. And then he married her. The fact that a back-up dancer from Fresno managed to seduce the most sought-after woman in America (at the time), lock her down with two children, and then drive her to the madhouse is pretty impressive. I'm no expert, but Kevin might be the best loser in history.

Maybe this is an exaggeration (it's not), but he certainly secured top position on the moocher's food chain, next to children and Kato Kaelin. The only way Mr. Spears could have topped this success would have been if Britney managed to stab herself in the jugular with that umbrella as she fended off the paparazzi, leaving her estate to Kevin. Death by insanity just wasn't in the cards for the pop princess. Maybe next time, K-Fed. Maybe next time.

How a non-contributing zero managed to come out on top of that hilariously horrific marriage, is beyond comprehension. This is someone who left his pregnant girlfriend for Bentleys, Cristal and VonDutch hats. And after two blissful barefoot years, two boys, and two rehab stints the soul mates finally called it quits. Via text message. And the great "meh" was heard around the world.

Luckily for everyone but Britney, it didn't end there. Psychotic would be a positive description of the chaos that ensued after their break-up. We all sat back and watched our beloved southern belle unravel. From shaving her head, to throwing milkshakes at paparazzi, her famous hit and run, and the best and most deliberate vag-shot to date, the pop star continued to entertain America in the most epic meltdown of all time. We failed Britney.

In the meantime, fat Kevin was granted temporary custody of their two children and joyfully collected child support, which we all know was spent mostly on bad wardrobe choices and his carb intake.

* * *

Lydia and I swapped numerous emails through the affair. Mostly consisting of patronizing insults, silly vitriol and the overall understanding that we hated each other. I was becoming increasingly cattier. Although the Co-dependent continuously told me that they were either on the outs or finished, I always knew better. But I was more caught up in winning than I was interested in the details. Looking back, I'm not even sure I really wanted to be with him, but I definitely didn't want him to be with Lydia.

"*There are many things that we would throw away if we were not afraid that others might pick them up.*" —Oscar Wilde

The Codependent continued to message me from time to time after they'd moved to Hope. Usually he was in his workshop, claiming that he was hiding from Lydia. At least that was his story. And sometimes he would show up unannounced late at night, throwing pebbles at my bedroom window. I'd entertain him on a friendly level, but by this time I'd moved on.

Their relationship didn't survive much longer once I disappeared. Eventually she probably grew tired of his shit, packed up, left Hope and moved to Fuck-it. At least I assume that's what happened. Maybe she missed me, who knows? You can only support someone and their dream of never having a real job for so long before you start to resent them for eating all your food.

* * *

I've always been plagued with a strange curse. Once I finally let go of a toxic relationship and I'm finally in a positive, forward-moving headspace, they come back. The Jock did. The Cheater did a few years after I'd moved to the city and he'd broken up with Jane. And the Codependent tried once Lydia kicked him out. It takes a long time for me to allow myself to let go of someone I love, but once I do, the chapter is closed. If it didn't work the first time, I'm of the mind that it never will.

I don't think I'll ever come back from the lie I told. It will embarrass and haunt me for as long as I'm breathing atop this mortal coil. Choosing to be candid about it was one of the hardest decisions I think I've ever made. Every time I think about it, I cringe and turtle. It's like checking your phone after blacking-out on Sangria and Tequila shots and you find the unsolicited, sloppy-drunk-texts you sent to your hot coworker. The whole thing was selfish and it was mad and it has come with a price. Lying your way onto someone's radar is a pretty low position in life. I was so caught up in the game that I failed to remember it wasn't just about me.

I couldn't compete with Lydia. There was no competition. The Codependent was at a point in his life where he didn't want what I was able to provide, he wanted to be provided for. I couldn't offer that. But he was probably right when he said he was afraid of holding me back from living my life, despite whatever selfish intention was hidden in that message. I was 20 years old. I had a lot of living ahead of me and every year I've had since him has been greater than the 19 I had before him: the people I've met, the places I've gone, the experiences I've acquired, none of it would have ever happened. I'd probably still be writing that aimless memoire, jerking off to my own meaningless existence. But I mean, who knows, maybe that's what I'm doing now.

At the end of the day, I like to look at this whole debacle as though I saved Lydia from shaving her head and showing her vagina to the world. I could have lingered around longer and made it more dramatic, after all she was well on her way to the loony bin. Had I pushed a little harder, dug a little deeper, she may have actually wound up there. My forfeit saved her integral sanity. She should probably thank me. Though call me crazy, but I have a feeling that's off the table.

So, you're welcome, Lydia.

"(Insert self-deprecating imagery here)" —Dave "Oderus Urungus" Brockie

CHAPTER 5:
THE ADDICT

"It's a mistake to confuse pity with love."

—Stanley Kubrick

AFTER Richard, I bounced around the dating scene for a while. I guess I was looking to reunite with who I was before I unlocked the door to Wonderland. In doing so, I found an old friend, an old friend turned new lover. He was a musician from my hometown who'd also moved to Vancouver. We hung out on a regular basis. We'd spend our evenings at local shows, hiding in the far corners of dark venues, drinking wine and discussing absolutely everything. Warren was tortured, probably more than I was. It sounds pretentious, but this was before the tortured musician concept was reduced to a meme—thanks, hipster pandemic.

We were equally heartbroken, trudging through the stages of moving on, but we found a familiarity in each other. And we both began to find ourselves again. Warren's experience far surpassed mine, so I listened to him, enjoying every anecdote. Before anything romantic, we were friends and we cared for each other in the ways we needed to be cared for. We spent months discussing the woes of our missteps and wayward hearts, cauterizing our old wounds.

Eventually we went our separate ways. Warren fell in love with his manager and the rest is history. It was probably for the best, as I have no idea how we would have fared as a couple once we had nothing left to whine about.

After Warren, I dated a bartender, a sober bartender, possibly the only sober bartender on earth. Chad was an attractive, fun-loving bimbro (if that's not a word yet, I'm coining it). His Facebook profile photos were mostly of him shot-gunning beer with fellow frat boys, floating down the river in a cowboy hat, or with his family, dressed in obnoxious ugly Christmas sweaters, smiling like a group of turds. Chad's interests consisted mostly of weight training, inspirational quotes and the pyramid scheme he was convinced would make him rich one day. This relationship was short-lived.

We ended it after about month, and I mean it was probably for the best. Trying to explain words like ambiguous and superfluous to someone whose desktop wallpaper was a photo of a dolphin jumping into the sunset alongside the quote "Be the change you wish to see in this world," was probably a losing battle.

Once Chad and I called it quits, I decided to enjoy being single for a while. A while turned into a long two-year dating hiatus, where I basically just slept around with a bunch of different people, playing dodgeball with the clap.

I was single for so long after my relationship with Richard ended that my mother would constantly call to ask me if I'd turned gay. I'd kept Warren, Chad, and my trail of slutty endeavors from her, so she was convinced that the only possible reason for my isolation was that I'd started batting for the other team. I was just someone who took time to get over someone, to understand why it went wrong. Unlike my mother, who quickly moved from penis to penis like an orangutan swinging through the jungle in *Planet Earth*.

* * *

I began working at a little dive bar downtown in the fall of 2008. One Friday night, I was carefully flipping through the CD covers in the jukebox during my shift when I heard a whisper over my shoulder.

"LA Woman," the voice requested.

I spun around and before I had an opportunity to jump down the stranger's throat, we locked eyes and curiously watched each other for a moment in silence.

"Excuse you," I asserted, finally snapped out of his Jedi mind trick. I turned back to the jukebox.

He leaned into me. He was warm and he smelled like clean laundry. As he drew closer, his lips grazed my ear. "Just play my song," he whispered.

And as quickly as he appeared, he disappeared.

Eugene was something mysterious. He was unreadable and his presence haunted you. He was the type of person who loved and hated fully, there was no in-between because he was uncomfortable in the balance. His gaze could bore through a vault. He would look at you so intensely that for a minute, as you watched his furrow brow chisel a permanent line into his forehead, you would lose all sense of awareness.

He continued to watch me throughout the night. We'd awkwardly lock eyes every now and then before exchanging feeble smiles. One of the other servers convinced me to give him my number, so I wrote it down on a napkin and waited for him to approach me again. As the night drew to a close and the lights went up, the bar folk slowly dispersed. I noticed Eugene following a group of people out the door. Just as he was about to exit, he turned around. His eyes darted around the restaurant before finding me and he sprang in my direction.

"This might be offside..." he began but I cut him off mid-sentence when I slipped him the crumpled-up piece of paper that I'd been fidgeting with for the past two hours. He laughed, "My name is Eugene, by the way."

I smiled and he started toward the front door to catch up with his friends.

"I'll call you," he yelled as he approached the exit. He looked down at the piece of paper he'd peeled open. "Jordan!"

He was sweet, a little weird maybe, but sweet.

I didn't hear from him over the following few days so I decided against obsessing over Eugene. I chalked the mysterious guy in the bar up to another patron/waitress strikeout.

I was working a dayshift the following Sunday when a young guy in a black sweatshirt and baseball hat walked in the front door and up to bar.

"Is Jamie working?" he asked the bartender.

"There's no Jamie who works here," she replied. I glanced up and recognized Eugene. The bartender looked over to me, just in time to notice that I knew the stranger. "We do have a Jordan, though. Is that who you're looking for?" she asked him.

"Yes! That's her!" he proclaimed, not realizing I might have heard him. "I was drunk on Friday. I lost her number and couldn't remember her name." The bartender raised her indifferent expression toward me. He turned around to follow her gaze, realizing I heard the forgotten name fiasco. His cheeks turned flush with embarrassment. "Shit," he muttered. But I heard that too. He raised his hand in a defeated wave.

I laughed.

"I lost your number," he admitted as I walked toward him.

"I heard," I responded.

He extended his arm to shake my hand, "I'm Eugene. Did we go over that already? I live downtown, I have a dog named Betty, I enjoy coffee at midnight and pizza for breakfast," he said, trying to break the ice.

"I'm Jordan. I live over the bridge, I prefer cats and I'm allergic to pizza, coffee, and forgetful drunks," I responded facetiously.

He chuckled.

I escorted him to an empty table in my section to chat. I signaled to the other server that I was going to take a quick break.

We chatted for a few minutes before making plans to meet for a drink the following Thursday after a show at the Railway Club that I had already committed to. We exchanged numbers and then he was gone.

* * *

Four days later, he swaggered in through the pub doors, intensely shifting his gaze around the room. He looked like a predator. And I was totally into it. (This is generally one of those times where you should probably reevaluate your hardwiring system.)

He propped himself next to me at the bar and ordered a beer. We talked for hours. Eugene listened as much as he spoke. He paid attention and genuinely showed interest. There was no arrogance. He was between jobs, floating around post-breakup. I could tell Eugene had a dark past. He was passionate and intense but a little confused and irate, like that one goth friend in high school who introduced you to TOOL and whip-its.

I've always been a magnet for men who are tattooed, jobless and basically going nowhere in life. The lost boy I could reunite with his family. Some people might refer to this as saintly, but most would call it delusional.

The closing lights turned on and, like a desperate Australian drifter on an expired working Visa, I brought him home with me. Shamelessly preying on the predator.

The next morning, he asked if I wanted to go for brunch. I tried to wheel around it. Honestly, I wasn't interested, but something about his reaction when I declined made me feel like a monster. We were obviously in different stages of our lives and I was hoping this wouldn't evolve past a one-night sort of thing. But I guess I was guilted into brunch. And then into paying for it.

He called the following day. I agreed to meet him for a bite that afternoon. I suppose I was lonely. I suppose he started to grow on me, along with the idea of financial burden.

Eugene was sweet, but he wasn't boyfriend material. He was living in a hostel at the time because his ex-girlfriend had kicked him out, so I mean, that's probably one reason. And because he was technically homeless, he was forced to pawn his dog off on a friend while he searched for a place to live. And a job.

Neither of these red flags seemed to grab my attention. Nor did his attempt to convince me to let him move in to my apartment. Saintly quickly deescalated to stupid and like a full-blown idiot, I began to date Eugene.

After a month of perpetual sleepovers, I began to put pressure on him to start looking for somewhere to live. A few interviews and viewings later, he eventually found a place about a ten-minute walk from my apartment.

Soon after moving in, he started a new job and collected his dog.

Right when things appeared to be leveling out for the vagrant, he decided to tell me that he was in love with me. This terrified me. What was he thinking? You don't make a commitment like that after four weeks. Do you? Hell, I could barely commit to brunch.

I didn't say it back. In fact, he continued to tell me he loved me for three months before I begrudgingly returned the sentiment. It was awkward and unnatural, like Hitler's mustache. I may have even rolled my eyes. It felt like a moral obligation to appease his sanity. Let me rephrase, it was most definitely a moral obligation to appease his sanity.

I quickly peeled away the layers to Eugene's past and indeed it was dark. His family was absent, extended and confusing. He'd never been well taken care of and as a result, he struggled with a plethora of addictions. He decided to kick heroin when he found out that an ex-girlfriend of his had been diagnosed with HIV. It was muddy. Moreover, my inner hypochondriac forced thoughts of AIDS into my consciousness every time I saw him naked. Eugene didn't have AIDS. I'd just convinced myself that he might.

* * *

Late one night, I received a phone call from Eugene as I was getting home from work. Betty's paw was swollen and she was in a lot of pain. I told him to just try to make her comfortable for the night and we would take her to the vet the following day.

I showed up the next morning with coffee around 9 AM. Eugene was disheveled and frantic. I could tell he hadn't slept. His eyes were bloodshot and he was exhausted, his hair was a mess and he was in the same clothes I saw him in the previous day. He threw on a hat and carried Betty out to the car.

When we arrived at the veterinary clinic, there was panic in the receptionist's eyes as she looked at Betty's paw. It was red and had grown to the size of a baseball. Eugene was too distracted to notice her response, but I knew the result was going to be morose.

The vet saw us right away and without a stroke of hesitation, he told Eugene he was certain Betty had cancer. Eugene tried to hold back his tears as the vet listed our options. He wanted to take an x-ray to be certain, so we waited.

Sure enough, it was cancer. Betty either needed immediate amputation to attempt to stop the cancer from spreading or she would have to be put down. I asked him how much the surgery would cost.

The vet hesitated, looking up at the two of us with sheer sadness. "Twelve-hundred dollars," he responded.

Eugene broke down which caused the veterinarian to choke up. There I was, standing in an animal clinic between two grown men as they cried over this poor dog. I looked down at Betty, lying on the cold examination table with her head slumped between her paws. She peered up at me with her big, helpless, brown eyes.

"Listen," the vet started, "I'm willing to wave my labor. I'll cut the price in half to just the cost of anesthesia and equipment. I'll do the surgery for free. For six hundred I can get her on my table this afternoon."

I knew Eugene still couldn't afford that. "I'll pay it," I blurted. Surprised, Eugene glanced over. "You can pay me back when you can," I said to him.

"I can't let you do that, it's a lot of money," he replied. "I'll figure out a way to pay for it."

"You heard him, she needs the surgery now and it feels like this offer has an expiry." I looked at the vet. "Who do I pay?"

"My receptionist will take care of it," he said as he directed me to the front desk. He spoke with her for a brief moment, explaining the cost breakdown.

I handed her $600 in cash. She looked at the wad of money and snickered, "Let me guess, you're a waitress?"

I shot her a pantomimed eye roll. Congratulations idiot, you win $600 for your outstanding guess. I walked back into the vet's office where Eugene was huddled on the floor, cradling his pet. We waited about half an hour before the vet returned to the office to prep Betty for surgery. Eugene held her as his tears soaked her furry forehead. She huddled close to him, whimpering.

The vet whisked her away to the back room. Eugene reached for a tissue on a nearby shelf. His face was red and his eyes were swollen, "Thank you for doing this. I won't forget this. You're saving her life." He started to well up again.

I stood there uncomfortably before reaching out to give him a hug. As previously mentioned, I'm terrible in these situations. I would rather fall through the earth and be burned alive by the outer core than console someone. When someone's loved one dies, my idea of trying to help is explaining how death is life's only certainty. Sometimes I even start to ramble on about how there probably isn't an afterlife. Or a God. It's generally best if I just stay away from funerals or any situation where people are feeling emotional.

* * *

So on went life with tripod Betty. She adapted quickly. A few days of self-pity and confusion, but it wasn't long before she was back to her old self, hobbling around on her three good legs.

While the dog got better, our relationship grew worse. We started arguing a lot, mostly over Eugene finding a stable job. But the arguments escalated into a variety of nonsense. I started to grow sexually stale. I wasn't really interested in sleeping with him anymore and he noticed so we fought about that. We fought about money. We fought about his jealousy. Oh, did we fight about his jealousy. Eugene carried immense disdain for my male friends. Everyone rubbed him the wrong way and he didn't hide it. Jealously doesn't bode well with me. My independent nature requires personal space and trust. Like I said, I'm a cat person.

* * *

That winter, I took a trip to Cuba with my best friend. Wi-Fi was non-existent there at the time (probably still is), so I was unable to keep in touch with him over the week. I'd been to Cuba a couple years prior, so I warned him that I would be off the grid until I was back.

When I returned home the following week, he told me he had decided to sell the hockey tickets I bought him for Christmas because I didn't email him while I was away.

On top of his mountain of negative character traits, he was also a bad listener. Eugene was flippant and needy. He suffocated me. He wanted to be around me every day. It drove me insane. I felt obligated to invite him to social gatherings and dinners, which would always end in a fight, generally because other males would attend. I started to grow tired of his shit and wanted out of the relationship. I worked to devise an amicable breakup situation. Mostly because I wanted the $600 he owed me, but also to avoid being chopped up, limb-by-limb and stuffed into a chest freezer, because he was actually that obsessed with me.

However, every time I attempted to encourage a conversation about our terrible relationship, Eugene the Spaz turned it into a pity party for himself and I caved, kyboshing the topic. I felt sorry for him. I was all he had and I knew any way I sliced it, he would cause a scene, one that would cost me $600. I decided to tough it out for a while longer.

One night as we were lying in bed watching a movie at his house, he began to rub my thigh. I casually squirmed and he stopped. A few minutes later he rested his hand back on my leg and slowly crept up my thigh. I swatted his hand away. I know this sounds harsh. It was. I admit that it was a terrible response to his advances. By this point I was so disinterested in a sexual relationship with him that I acted organically and without considering the fallout. Well, he exploded. As any emotionally sound human being probably would.

"What the fuck was that?" he burst at me.

I jumped as his anger boomed from behind me. "I, I'm sorry. I just reacted. I'm not feeling well," I shakily responded as I turned around to face him.

"You know, you haven't been feeling well for a while now," he snapped, using air-quotes.

I stared at him blankly.

"What the hell is your problem? Do you not want to be with me anymore?" he continued.

I continued to stare. I had nothing to say. I should have been honest but I was too annoyed to satisfy his outburst. "I don't know," I finally replied.

"Well, what the fuck is that supposed to mean?" he sat up.

"I just mean." I took a deep breath and before I had a chance to consider the odds. I gambled. "You're constantly fighting with me. You hate my friends. You hate everything you're not involved in. You're an asshole when I need space. I pay for everything. You're still working odd jobs. You're 33. Pull your life together. It's unattractive," I fired back. I'd said it, unloading everything that had fueled my distance from him.

He shot up out of bed as I sat up. "Are you fucking kidding me?" he was screaming by this point. "I put you first all the time. I'm trying to make ends meet. I'm trying to sort everything out. Who the fuck do you think you are?"

I stood up and reached for my clothes. He stood up after me.

"Where do you think you're going?" he screamed in my ear, dangerously close.

"I think it's best if I stay at my place tonight. We can decompress and discuss this tomorrow," I said to him as I fastened my jeans and pulled my shirt over my head. I started to gather my purse and my belongings.

He stared at me in disbelief as I turned to exit the room and flew down the stairs. I reached the front entrance and out of nowhere, he came shooting down the stairs and threw his body into the door as I'd begun to open it. The door slammed shut. He locked it and glared at me, inches from my face. "You aren't leaving," he said through gritted teeth.

"Oh, I'm leaving. Get away from the door, Eugene," I said sternly, glaring back at him. In that moment, I watched his nose flare as his eyeballs produced a glimmer of evil in the light. He was about to lose control and I suddenly felt very unsafe. "Calm down," I directed.

"You fucking bitch." He pushed me backwards away from the door. I stumbled before I caught my step. "Don't tell me to calm down!" he ordered. I looked up at him and for a minute I could have sworn he was going to kill me. His rage filled the room and haunted the entire house. A demon I'd never seen spilled from his orifices as he stood in the entrance. I reached for him in an attempt to calm him down. He pushed my hands away.

He started screaming and everything began to blur. I couldn't even comprehend *what* he was screaming. Betty was barking as Eugene began to back me into the kitchen. I watched his eyes as they darted around the room before stopping on something atop the counter. I followed his gaze to the old hand-me-down knife block. This person was going to end my life. In this shitty house, in front of his three-legged dog, over a little rejection. How disappointing. This was not the life my mother had planned for me. And this was nothing like the death I'd planned for myself. I've always pictured myself croaking at a more appropriate age, in a slightly less dramatic manner. Maybe somewhere public, like my favorite diner as I'm reading the paper. Just like that. Face first into my scrambled eggs moments before the surly, middle-aged waitress approaches the table to fill my coffee. This was nothing even close to that. I hadn't become famous enough to die at the hand of my psychopath boyfriend. No one would remember this. (Therein lies the real tragedy.)

I started to panic. I had to find a way out of this so I did what any self-respecting, 23-year-old female would do. I started to cry.

And like a typical man, he crumbled. He snapped out of his frenzy and immediately begged forgiveness. "I'm sorry. I love you," he said. "I didn't mean to scare you. I was upset. Please don't hate me. Please don't leave. I'm so sorry."

I was confused. I expected him to quit the somewhat impressive Norman Bates act, not profusely apologize. Honestly, I was more disturbed by his bipolar flip than I was over his initial temper tantrum. This was a real pickle. Anything I said would set him off. I decided to play nice. I accepted his apology and in turn apologized for denying his advances. I stuck by my lie and said I really hadn't been feeling well.

I knew I couldn't leave. I followed him back up the stairs to his room, where I slept with one eye open, and only one-half of my dignity for the rest of the night.

Asshole Rating: 9.5 Because crazy assholes often become accidental murderers.

* * *

A few weeks passed and things were getting a little better. We were fighting a lot less and he started to give me a little breathing room. And I mean, I was just happy to be breathing at all.

My mother came to town for a visit that March. When she met Eugene, she was unsure of him. Okay that's an understatement. I believe her words were "controlling leech." In her defense, she was pretty dead on.

On her last night, Eugene was supposed to meet us for dinner to try to redeem himself. But he never showed up. It was very unlike him not to attend something I'd invited him to, especially dinner with my mother. I tried calling him numerous times. His phone went straight to voicemail. We finished dinner without him, but I continued to call him throughout the night. Finally, my mother told me to stop.

"Jordan, the guy is an idiot. I don't want to sound mean, but you're better than him. You need to cut this one loose." She was always an advocate for brutal honesty. I decided to leave it alone for the night.

I woke up early the following morning and decided to try calling again. It went to voicemail. Before opting to go to his house and find out what was going on, I weighed the options. What if I found him with another girl? How would I react? Did I possess the ability to act calmly in that situation? I needed to know.

Twenty minutes later, I was unlocking his front door with the spare key he'd given me. The house was still. It appeared that no one was home. The floor creaked under my boots as I tiptoed through the front entrance. I felt like I was break and entering. I quietly made my way up the stairs to find Eugene's bedroom door closed. My heart started to beat faster as I approached the door, slowly building up the courage to open it.

CHAPTER 5: THE ADDICT

Finally, I took a deep breath and I turned the handle. The door opened to the dimly lit bedroom. Eugene was asleep on top of his bed, fully dressed and alone. I was positive I was going to find someone with him. But as I started to feel an overwhelming sigh of relief, I remembered that this prick just blew off dinner with my mother. Fuck him.

I walked over to the side of his bed and kicked the mattress. He rolled into consciousness. "What the fuck!" he protested, blinking as I came into focus. "Why did you just kick me?"

"I didn't kick you, I kicked the mattress," I snapped, "Where the fuck were you last night?"

"Huh?" he asked, confused.

"Last night, dinner with my mother. Remember? Where were you?"

"Oh. I was," he paused, thinking of an alibi. "At work. My phone died," he blurted.

I laughed condescendingly because the idea of him having a job was so hilarious that I couldn't control it. "You were working? Really? Doing what?"

He scrambled, "I got a last-minute call for a camera job on a commercial," he explained. I knew he was lying.

"Oh really? What commercial?" I quizzed.

"Some stupid car commercial. It was a long day. I didn't get home until really late and then I passed out," he attested.

"Right," I responded, unconvinced. "Well why don't you call me with the truth once you're up." I stormed out of the room, down the stairs and out the front door.

My mother left that night. After seeing her off at the airport, I returned home. When I arrived, Eugene was sitting on the cement wall near the entrance to my building.

"What are you doing here?" I asked.

"I have to talk to you about something. I wanted to do it in person," he replied.

"I'm only interested if you're here to tell the truth. Otherwise, go away." I brushed him off.

"I'm going to tell you the truth. But you aren't going to like what I have to say. Can I come up?"

I looked at him curiously. Something was up. Something I hadn't prepared for. He was broken and ashamed and not really in the I'm a cheating douche way.

"Fine." I hesitated as I unlocked the front door. He followed me up to my apartment.

We walked through the front door and into the dining room. He sat down at the table as I grabbed a bottle of wine off the counter. I sat down across from him and poured myself a glass without offering him one. I took a long sip as I looked up at him. "Well?"

"This isn't easy," he said. "I've been struggling with something for many years now, and it's something you're not going to understand."

"Try me."

"Okay…" he trailed off as he shuffled in his seat. "I missed out on dinner because I was smoking crack." He watched as I studied him. "I've been battling a crack addiction for longer than I can remember."

I think I might have gone into shock because I just stared into dead space while I crawled inside my own head and my inner monologue took over. *"Who the fuck has a crack addiction?"* I thought. *"Is that still a thing? Like, for someone who isn't homeless? I mean he was homeless, kind of, but not in a junkie sort of way. Am I dating a closet junkie? Is that worse than dating a closet gay? Does he let other closet gays suck his dick for crack money? Is crack a needle drug? Oh God. He must have AIDS. Great, now I definitely have AIDS."*

He continued, breaking up my inner meltdown. "Once in a while, when I'm stressed out, I go on a bender. I shut off my phone. I shut off all communication and the addiction takes over. I can't control it and I need help," he said calmly.

He wasn't lying and yet I stared at him in disbelief. And then I did the worst possible thing you can do in this type of situation. I laughed.

Naturally, he grew angry. "This isn't funny. Why are you laughing?"

"I'm sorry, I just. I assumed you were cheating and this is just… so much worse." I tried to straighten out. "I'm sorry, I'm not laughing at you. It's just the way I react to incredibly unbelievable situations."

He looked confused.

"I don't know how I'm supposed to respond to this. I can't be with someone who has a crack addiction, Eugene. This is something you need to get right with," I said.

"I know. I want to. I want you to help me," he replied.

"I don't really know how I'm supposed to help you. This isn't exactly in my realm of expertise. Aren't there people for this?" I suppose I'm not the most sensitive person on earth. And by that I mean that he probably would have been better off talking to a shoe.

"I just need your support. I'm going to see a counsellor. I've already made appointments. But I need you in my corner," he begged.

I wanted to end it right there. But he was desperate, and broken, and he could even have AIDS.

Okay, just to be clear, if all the other signs hadn't previously lead me to the conclusion that maybe it's time to reevaluate my relationship, this should probably have been the one. Yet there I was, feeling sad and sorry for him, obligated to continue my quest to mend the broken boy. I didn't love him anymore. I knew I didn't want to be with him, I knew he was dragging me down, I knew he wasn't capable of being in a balanced relationship and most of all, I knew he was out of his goddamned mind. But I felt responsible for him. I couldn't turn my back on an addict. I was all he had. And I mean 600 bucks is 600 bucks.

Crazy Level: 1.5 Because I'd become the asshole.

* * *

So, on it dragged. I began to grow distant again. I would make plans with my friends that he wasn't invited to and I took on extra shifts at work to stay occupied. Eugene grew increasingly impatient. He'd stuck to his meetings and claimed to be getting better. I cared for him deeply, but I looked at him as more of a friend. The friend you don't tell your other, cooler friends about.

I received a call from an old pal. Scotty, a country musician from Hamilton, is like an older brother to me. He's the type of person who fills a room, in both personality and hair. His pompadour hairstyle from 1955 is one to be revered as he regales you with tales about life on the road and the mafia kingpin he grew up next door to.

He'd called to invite me to meet him in Calgary where his tour would end. He knew I was struggling with Eugene and needed a break, so I agreed. A quick jaunt to Calgary was exactly what the doctor ordered. We spent our days gallivanting around the city, barhopping around his favorite watering holes. And we spent our nights laughing over drinks with wisecracking country-folk between Scotty's sets. It was what I needed: a weekend listening to strange stories, meeting new people, and drinking whiskey with my favorite accomplice.

I woke up that Sunday morning to loud ringing. I turned over in my hotel room bed and reached for my phone on the nightstand. The bed adjacent to mine was empty and unmade. Scotty was up, blow-drying the pompadour in the bathroom.

I looked at the call display before answering. Eugene.

"Hello?" I answered.

"Why didn't I hear from you last night? When are you coming home?" he ripped into me without as much as a simple greeting.

"Why are you calling me so early? I was at Scotty's show last night. I told you that before I went out. I'm coming home this afternoon," I snapped back. At this time, I'd quietly moved into the hallway to avoid bringing any attention to my drama. I sat on the orangey-brown carpet, looking down the hallway as the maid pulled a stack of towels off her cart and then disappeared into a room. I scanned the corridor. Wall-to-wall vomit. This place was tackier than a Russian mail-order bride.

"What the hell is wrong with you? You could at least keep in touch. How do you think this makes me feel?" Eugene fired.

"Chill out. I texted you last night. You're acting like a baby. Stop it."

"A baby? I'm acting like a baby because I give a shit about you?" His voice was so loud that I pulled the phone away from my ear. The maid reappeared at the end of the hallway carrying a bundle of dirty sheets.

She plopped them into the basket attached to the cart and reached for fresh ones.

"Settle down and stop yelling at me. You're acting crazy," I whispered.

"Crazy? Do you want to see cra–"

I hung up the phone. This was insane. What was wrong with this guy? I turned off my ringer and stepped back into the hotel room. Scotty was sitting in a chair on the far side of the suite, looking out the window. He turned to face my direction as the door clicked behind me, "Listen honey, I know this is none of my business, but I have to be honest with you here." He looked concerned, "This ain't the guy for you."

"So you heard," I said. "I'm sorry, I stepped out to avoid that."

"I heard. And it breaks my heart to see you upset over some bitter asshole. You have a life and you are always going to have a life. If he can't understand that you're independent, then he's got to go. Because from where I'm standing, it's only going to get worse from here." Scotty's words were soft and filled with empathy.

Eugene continued to call until I boarded the plane and turned my phone off.

When I landed, I decided it was best to leave the Eugene drama alone for the night. I went out for a few drinks with my friend Jenn instead. I needed to assess the pros and cons to this dumpster fire of a relationship. Eugene hadn't called since I landed. I assumed he was angry by this point. And honestly, I was okay with that.

I woke up early the next morning to tension in my back from a stressful sleep. Something wasn't right. I reached for my phone. No missed calls. I dialed Eugene's number. Straight to voicemail. Something was definitely off. I jumped out of bed and threw on some clothes.

I spotted Jenn asleep on the couch as I made my way to the kitchen for a glass of water. I'd forgotten that she'd decided to stay over. She woke up as I fumbled around the fridge. "What time is it?" she asked as she turned to me. She realized I was dressed and she changed her questioning. "Where are you going?"

I finished pouring the glass of water and slid the water jug back onto the shelf. I stepped out of the kitchen and between sips of water I casually unloaded the news. "Eugene's phone is off. I'm going to walk down there to check it out."

She looked concerned. "Give me a minute to get up. I'll drive you." The drive to Eugene's house was filled with silence and suspense. Once we pulled up outside, Jenn lit a cigarette. "I'm going to wait here," she said.

I thanked her as I pulled the spare key out of my pocket and slipped out the passenger side. A knot formed in the pit of my stomach when I approached the front door. I knew how this was going to end. I inserted the key into the keyhole and cautiously turned the lock. I winced when the deadbolt clicked and then carefully popped the door ajar as déjà vu engulfed me. I decided that tiptoeing was pointless. I shut the front door behind me and jogged up the stairs. I stood outside his bedroom for a moment, flooded with anger and yet fearful of the incubus I knew was on the other side.

I was about to turn the handle and open the door when something weird happened. All the anger suddenly floated away like a leaf caught in a burst of wind. My anger transformed into acceptance. And I was calm, relieved even. The house was dead quiet. With a deep breath, I swung the door open. And as I suspected, there he was, face down in his clothes. There was no incubus, just a broken man presenting my broken relationship.

I shook my head as he began to stir.

"What are you doing here?" he croaked as he rubbed his eyes.

"A better question is, what are *you* doing here?" I said. He froze, staring up at me. He was ashamed and knew he couldn't lie. There was a long pause. I calmly smiled at him. "This isn't working and I can't be a crutch for your addiction anymore. This is your life and it's sinking. I'm not prepared to go down with that ship. I've done what I can. You need help that I can't provide and I really hope you get it." I turned and flew down the stairs before he had a chance to respond.

"What's going on?" Jenn asked as I got back in the car. My eyes began to water. "Jordan, what is going on?" she persisted.

I didn't answer her. I'd hidden Eugene's secret from everyone. He was anything but stable, and my friends weren't strangers to his insanity, but this would have painted the worst possible picture. I didn't think he deserved that. This was Eugene's struggle. It was his story to tell.

* * *

Over the following week, Eugene would come by the bar, teary-eyed and desperate to fix things, but I refused to budge. I was amicable and friendly because there was no need for animosity between us, but also because I still felt like he was crazy enough to kill me in my sleep. And maybe I secretly hoped I might see that $600 he owed me.

When he realized that I couldn't be swayed with tears, as a last-resort attempt to get back together, he would show up at my apartment with strange gifts. One day he gave me a half-dead rosemary plant. A few weeks after that, he showed up with an industrial iPod speaker. I'm 95 percent certain he stole it from a construction site, but I didn't ask any questions. I think he felt that it made us even for Betty's surgery.

That was the afternoon that I parted with the money. Eugene had many demons and many debts that he was beholden to, and I knew this was the only way I could help absolve him of one of them. We've managed to remain friends on social media with minimal interaction, though I had to unfollow him when I realized that he was an Infowars subscriber.

It was probably for the best. The Downtown East Side is no place for a hypochondriac.

CHAPTER 5.5:
ENDURANCE

"Love? What is it? Most natural painkiller."

—William S. Burroughs, spoken like a guy who is about
to murder his wife.

MY experience with the Addict was something extraordinary. And terrifying. He was passionate, dismissive, loving, controlling, simple, and complicated all wrapped into a tightly wound ball of confusion. He was like a Rubik's Cube that was unsolvable because someone had moved the stickers around on it. The medical term for this is bipolar. He was also clingy and he needed me more than I needed him—two extremely unattractive qualities in a man. Our relationship lasted about six months longer than it should have. Because at 22 years old everything has a price, even your sanity. In my case, that price appeared to be $600.

Every time I wanted to end the relationship, something upsetting or traumatic would happen to him and I would feel indebted to help him through it. It was a sad, perpetual cycle of pity and assumed obligation. But the Addict knew this. He knew my compassion ran deeper than his poor luck and he used that to his advantage. I remained wrapped in his turmoil because he knew I couldn't walk away from a wounded bird. He was a professional victim.

While the Addict definitely had wonderful qualities, okay, maybe that's a stretch, his constant quest for my attention and admiration became tiresome. He was a beast of burden and I allowed myself to be his emotional caddy. Truthfully, I wanted to be that for him. When you realize that your past relationships are essentially a collection of poor life choices and you've been tossed to the side more than you've been welcomed in, it feels good to be needed. But eventually I felt more like a mother figure to the Addict. I became a caretaker and a financial stool for an irresponsible teenager that refused to clean his room. What I didn't understand was that he didn't need a Norma to his Norman, he needed a Nancy to his Sid, someone who was willing to sink to his depths and absorb his demons rather than deflect them. I wasn't unraveled enough to be his equal.

I should probably mention that the Addict was also French. He didn't have much of an accent because he'd moved away from Montreal when he was quite young but it was the language he spoke when he was on the phone with his family members, and his dog seemed to understand him when he exploded into angry French diatribes. Now I'm not saying that French people have a predisposition for being a little crazy, but I'm sort of saying that French people have a predisposition for being a little crazy.

The Addict was a rare example of what happens when someone in the relationship is not only an asshole, but also crazy. It's an important dynamic to explore, as there is a small, yet significant number of crazy assholes out there. One may be right around the corner. The obvious areas of town to avoid would be: cheap restaurants, fetish clubs, welfare offices, hooker stands, French communities, and anywhere local drug dealers might hang out.

* * *

Sid Vicious is a good example of someone who clearly lost his Asshole Instruction Manual halfway through its use. This was a kid, yes a kid, with a severe heroin addiction. One that was primarily enabled by his own mother who was also a junkie. There was no hope for Sid. His entire existence on this earth was an ill-advised gamble against the odds. The tiny glimmer of hope that his association with the Sex

Pistols procured was quickly ripped out from under him when Nancy Spungen, slapped with Johnny Rotten's rejection, stumbled into his life.

Nancy was a woman of many weaknesses. Between being a stripper, a prostitute, a groupie, a junkie, and a dealer, she was also a diagnosed schizophrenic. Nauseating Nancy, as she was called, was strap-her-to-a-bed-in-a-white-padded-room crazy.

Between their pasts, bouts of domestic violence, and their insatiable appetite for heroin, what hope was there for either of these two? Especially together? Of course they were going to kill each other. There is no other course for that level of madness to take. (To be clear, Nancy didn't physically kill Sid, obviously I'm aware of that. But it's safe to assume her death was a catalyst for his overdose.)

There is speculation amongst their fellow industry friends and Sex Pistols fans that Sid didn't kill Nancy. Many said there was no way he was capable of committing murder and that he loved Nancy. Some believe it was a dealer who frequented their room at the Chelsea. Some think Nancy killed Nancy. Sid's recount of that fateful night changed a couple of times and that certainly didn't aid his defense. But as the destiny of a madman would have it, he overdosed while on bail, before the case even went to trial.

I watched an interview with a man who was friends with the couple. He told an infuriating story about the time Sid tied a belt around his cat's neck, lifted it off the floor and laughed as the life was mercilessly suffocated from the creature's body. As I've mentioned before, I don't fashion myself to be a killer connoisseur, but it doesn't take Shemar Moore and Joe Mantegna to make the connection between killing small animals and the criminal behavior of a sociopath. So, I attest, Sid most certainly was capable of committing murder whether he loved Nancy or not. He was also a cunt.

Sid Vicious may have been born a complete lunatic or he may have just inherited the characteristics of one through his addiction. Who knows? But any man capable of killing his pet is probably someone you want to avoid sharing a living space with.

Now for Nancy, she was a crazy heap of groupie trash that got caught up with an asshole musician, equally as messed up as she was. The only difference between the two was that Sid was undiagnosed. There was never an ounce of salvation for these two. Nancy never stood a chance because Sid had the forces of asshole on his side. It really didn't matter how crazy she was, her crazy couldn't outweigh his.

Nancy was destined to wind up lifeless under that sink on the bathroom floor of The Chelsea. In fact, Nancy's death probably brought her some level of fame that she smiles up at from whatever hellfire she wound up in in the afterlife. So, in all fairness, this was probably the best-case scenario for a junkie groupie.

* * *

I really have no evidence to support the claim that the Addict might have killed me that night in his kitchen. I can't imagine he would ever go through with something so insane. But assuming someone isn't capable of murder isn't really a gamble you want to take when it's your life on the betting table. He was an asshole and an addict, which brought along an unrivaled level of crazy. The only chance I felt I had at surviving the Addict's drama was to summon my own raging asshole from the depths. It was my only defense against his lunacy and the only way I knew how to deflect his attempts at reconciliation. Desperate relationships call for desperate measures.

When you find yourself trapped in the tornado of a crazy asshole, there is only one way out. You have to become the bigger asshole. But be warned, assholes are very delicate gremlins and need to be handled with care. You wouldn't want an irate, raging asshole running around and getting away from you, causing terror in an otherwise peaceful town. It's important that you exercise responsibility when unleashing your asshole. Don't get them wet or feed them after midnight.

And hey, if all else fails, cry. Men hate that.

CHAPTER 6:
THE PLAYBOY

"We are all crazy. Most women I know (including myself) have reacted the same way in certain high-emotional situations with men. The degree of crazy and how long the crazy lasts is usually what separates us."

—Mel Neale, my (unpaid) therapist.

ONCE Eugene and I were through, Jenn was adamant that I get back on the horse, so we partnered up and led each other on a month-long whoring carousel. We'd go out almost every night and prey on slews of men: randoms, bartenders, even friends, we didn't care. We were maniacs, feeding off each other's depravity because we'd both been cooped up in shitty relationships for the past year. We were finally single and ready to, well, orgy.

Don't get me wrong, we were having fun. But the fun came to a screaming halt the night we took home a set of cousins from the bar. Everything was going smoothly, Jenn hooked up with one of them on my couch, while I rolled around my bed with the other. It was a typical Thursday for us and after about an hour the apartment fell silent.

The following morning came with an irritating surprise, when I rolled over to find my late-night conquest still in the bed next to me. It's courtesy to quietly leave after a one-night stand. There's no need to stay over and make things awkward in the morning.

I looked around, trying to come up with a plan to get rid of the guy. I decided to go with the unsubtle, albeit foolproof approach; I faked a yawn and obnoxiously stretched my arms out, hitting him in the side of the face with the back of my hand. He groaned and slowly started to open his eyes.

"Oh, I didn't realize you were *still* here, I'm sorry about that," I said, trying to drop a get-the-fuck-out-of-here hint.

He rolled over onto his side and stared at me with these big puppy dog eyes and an annoying grin. "Good morning, you," he gushed.

I was confused. I'd just put emphasis on the word *still*, what was wrong with this picture? Time to go, bro. "Good morning. Don't you have anything to do today?" I said, slamming him with another hint.

"Nope. I actually just got back from traveling around Southeast Asia the past year and haven't gone back to work yet. I'm free to do whatever you want to do today."

I blinked at him in disbelief for about 10 full seconds. For someone who'd just spent a year traveling, he wasn't very self-aware. "Yeah see, that's not going to work for me today. I'm busy unfortunately," I said, secretly praying that Jenn would burst into the room and interrupt this skin-crawling exchange.

"Oh, that's okay," he trailed off. And just when I thought I'd been released from my personal hell, the worst possible verbal diarrhea spilled out of his mouth. "You know, your apartment is really spacious and I was thinking... I'm not really living anywhere at the moment, maybe I could crash here for a month?"

I stared at him like a deer in headlights. Was this happening? Did he get up early and huff my hairspray before this? I had willingly brought this degenerate into my house, so self-defense probably wouldn't be a believable cause for his death. Finally, I snapped back to reality. I shook my head, smiled and with all of the condescending coolness that I could muster, I just replied, "Nope."

* * *

After that, I decided it was time to hang up the push-up bra and take the spare underwear out of my purse. That encounter put the fear of God in me. I wasn't ready to start dating again. I didn't have the patience to become emotionally involved with someone else. Eugene had exhausted me. Though, he continued to make a valiant effort to creep under my skin and evoke jealousy by showing up at the bar I worked at every weekend with his new girlfriend. I laughed it off as my coworkers watched, eagerly waiting for me to throw a raw steak at him.

Apparently, our breakup was a lot worse for him. He eventually gave up, but not without an extremely pathetic fight. Eugene packed up his new girlfriend and the $600 tripod and moved across the country.

* * *

Soon after Eugene disappeared, I met Johnny through a mutual friend when we were out for drinks one night. Johnny was tall, graceless and slurring his words when he stumbled into the bar. I looked to Sam as the intoxicated mess approached us and slammed his body into the booth next to me. He reached for the bottle of beer in front of Sam, lifted it to his lips and tipped his head back. We watched while he feverishly gulped back the beer, finishing it off. As he tilted his head forward, he set the bottle back onto the table and let out a satisfied grunt. He looked at me and smiled with a drunken glaze that stretched from temple-to-temple. "Who are you?"

Sam interjected. "This is Jordan. Jordan, Johnny." I reached for a handshake. Johnny just stared at my hand as it wavered in the pocket of thick air that separated us. He didn't shake my hand. Instead, he reached behind my head with both hands and pulled my face toward him, aggressively kissing my forehead. Sam laughed. I was unimpressed and not nearly inebriated enough to deal with this barbarian.

After that first encounter, I found myself running into Johnny all over town. He was a bartender at a local strip club, so he too was a nightwalker and we mostly bumped into each other at concerts or the Roxy around last call. He was hardly charming. In fact, he was usually so wasted that he could barely string a sentence together. He wore wife beaters under button-ups and his hair was always slicked back to accentuate his muttonchops. He looked like the bastard lovechild of Pablo Escobar and Wolverine.

One night after work, we bumped into each other at a late-night hole-in-the-wall. We did a shot together and as the ugly lights flickered on, he asked for my number. I reluctantly gave it to him.

About a week later I started to receive illegible drunk text messages from him around two or three in the morning. I would either respond with something sassy or completely ignore them. There is only one reason on this earth to blast off a random text after midnight and you would have to be a puritan settler not to know what that reason is.

After a month of cat-and-mouse, he showed up unannounced at the bar while I was working one night. He ordered a drink and then without an iota of humility, he asked me why I played so hard to get. I just laughed and told him that his drunken booty calls were hardly inspiring. Before he left, he told me he would call me that week to take me to dinner. I didn't have an opportunity to decline, he was out the door and I had customers waiting for drinks.

The following Wednesday afternoon I received a text from him asking if I was available for dinner that night. I thought about the text for a few minutes, trying to decide how to respond. I definitely wasn't up for it, but I also didn't want to blatantly reject him. I decided to just ignore the message and respond a few hours later once the offer had likely expired. Sometimes the best response is no response, followed by a lie that you'd just woken up from a nap. So that's what I did.

He responded almost immediately and said that he would try again the following week. The guy was relentless. His advances were genuine and I sensed that, but he had a reputation. Johnny was a bit of a known womanizer. He dated girls for a while, until he got bored or something more sparkly (like a black stripper) came along. I'd dated enough emotionally stunted men by this point, I wasn't sure if I was interested in another round at that roulette table. But then again, I do hate myself.

A couple nights later, one of the servers and I decided to pop by the Roxy for last call after we finished closing up.

When we arrived, Johnny was leaning on the bar near the entrance, casually scanning the room while sipping on whiskey. I decided to go over and say hello. As we made our way through the messy crowd, shimmying between sweaty bodies, a flock of beautiful women approached him, intercepting my attempt to play nice. It was like watching a salmon being ripped apart by bloodthirsty crows—gorgeous, thin, drunk crows with incredibly well-proportioned breast implants. They all donned flashy outfits, exposing a sea of cleavage and flimsy morals. Their make-up was seamless and their weaves were styled perfectly. I stealthily slid into a spot at the bar about two meters away from the carnage, hoping I went unnoticed.

I ordered a drink and began to chat with my coworker. We were rehashing our night, discussing drunks and work politics, when I felt a tap on my right shoulder. I spun around. A smiling Johnny loomed over me.

"Hi! I saw you walk in. Why didn't you come say hi?" he quizzed.

"I was going to, actually. Before the gaggle swarmed you," I responded as I took a sip of whiskey. My coworker turned her back to us to chat with a few people who worked at a neighboring bar on the block. So there I was, forced to carry a conversation with the googly-eyed Columbian drug lord. We joked around, buying rounds of shots for each other as we laughed at the drunk girls stumbling around the bar, barefoot, dragging around poor European tourists under the assumption they were actually going to get laid, completely unaware that they would just wind up with a hefty cab cleaning fee after being drenched in their date's vomit. Johnny was sweet and we had a lot in common besides just a shared appreciation for schadenfreude.

As the lights came up and music went down, Johnny's boss approached us and asked if we wanted to go to the casino for bit. I was about to decline before Johnny spoke for both of us, "Yeah! We're in."

"I think I'll sit this one out guys. I should probably get home." I tried.

Johnny stared at me. "What could you possibly have to do tomorrow? I'm the one who has to get up for work in the morning. Come on. Just an hour. It'll be fun."

I looked at him, confused. What was he talking about? What bar job required a bartender to get up early for work? I shrugged it off and gave in.

We spent a little over an hour at the casino, watching Johnny lose about five hundred dollars before he finally decided that a third ATM withdrawal at 4 AM on a Monday was probably a poor life choice. The three of us decided to share a cab home. Johnny and I lived on the same side of town and his boss' place was along the way so we quickly dropped him off before carrying on over the bridge. Once we were alone, Johnny started to stumble over his words. I wasn't sure if it was nerves or the booze. Likely both.

"Do you want to come by my place for a drink? Or?" And there it was, that awkward moment. I knew it was a terrible idea. I shook my head to decline but he piped in again, "I mean just for one. We live so close and I'm not quite ready for bed yet."

Hook. Line. And sinker. Asshole. No one goes to a stranger's house at 4:30 in the morning to chitchat over a single drink.

I stared at him as the words escaped me, "Fine. For one."

He laughed, "Don't sound so excited." He gave the cab driver his address just in time to skip my exit.

His apartment was gorgeous and new, the opposite of mine. The kitchen was spacious with stainless steel appliances, marble counter tops and dark oak cupboards. It was an open-concept entertainment space. There were bar stools adjacent to the counter, separating the kitchen from the living room. His walls were decorated with framed band posters and his shelves held figurines, Mexican wrestling masks and old photographs of road trips and parties. He had weird trophies everywhere that I assumed were a part of his childhood. It was as if the room was telling the story of a man revolting against becoming an adult.

"Cool trophies, didn't realize you were a Kung-Fu artist," I said sarcastically as I walked around the room examining the collection. "Wait, who is Peter Hugh? And Andrew Thompson?" I looked closer at the plaques on the trophies as he poured our drinks in the kitchen. "Actually, why isn't your name on any of these?"

"Because they're not technically mine," he called from the kitchen. "I found most of them in a back alley when I was a kid. I thought they were cool, so I kept them," he responded.

I laughed hysterically. "You mean to tell me that you've been collecting the memories and lost achievements of strangers for the better part of your life?" I didn't know what was sadder, the idea that Andrew Thompson's parents realized his childhood karate achievements didn't really matter once he'd flown the coop, or that Johnny thought they did.

He walked over and handed me a glass of whiskey. He clinked my glass before taking a sip and looked at the trophies. "Are you always this cynical?" he asked.

"Actually, I'm usually worse," I responded with a smirk. "I have to say, nice apartment. For a drunk bartender with a knack for picking up innocent girls at the Roxy."

He laughed. "We both know that there are no innocent girls hanging out at the Roxy."

"Touché." I raised my glass toward him. We simultaneously drank as we shared a laugh at my expense.

He sat down on the worn leather couch and gestured for me to do the same. When I sat down on the opposite end of the couch, I caught a brief expression of disappointment in his eyes. But he quickly shook it off and we continued with our night, sharing funny stories as we nursed our drinks.

Eventually we ran out of small talk, so he did what any drunk guy would do at 5 AM with a lush in his apartment, he mumbled something incoherent before he shuffled closer to me and leaned in for the kill. I stiffened, because that's who I am, a social guppy. "I don't bite. Well, actually, I can't promise that," he said as he leaned in to kiss me again. This time, I was relaxed and prepared, so I kissed him back. It escalated quickly from there. By that I mean, in under a minute he had successfully removed my bra with his teeth.

"I'm not going to sleep with you," I finally said as he kissed my collarbone. He just laughed. Before long we were in his bedroom, naked.

And I was a hypocrite, filling my promise as the type of girl who hangs out at the Roxy.

The next morning, I woke up in a haze. Unaware of my surroundings, I sluggishly rolled over. When I slowly began to open my eyes, a body came into focus. I snapped to consciousness as a well of memories from the past eight hours flooded over me. Anxiety took the reigns and I was overwhelmed with the sudden urgency to bolt out of there. I stealthily crept out of the bed and tiptoed around the bedroom, collecting my clothing. I quietly exited the room and closed the door behind me. I scrambled to get dressed and searched around his apartment for my bra, but I couldn't find it anywhere. I began to panic when I realized it might be in his bedroom. I couldn't go back in there without waking him up. I continued to search but to no avail. Just as I was about to give up, committing to the idea of the shameful text I would have to send later, I spotted the bra on the floor, poking out from under the couch. Jackpot. I quickly picked it up and made way for the exit. I was home free. I unlocked the deadbolt and as I opened the front door, Johnny came flying out of his bedroom in his underwear.

"Where are you going?" he called, nearly out of breath.

I was annoyed and equally embarrassed that I'd been caught. I'd almost pulled off a perfect Houdini. I just wanted to go home and shower. I turned to face him. "As much as I'd love to stay and discuss last night, I should really get home."

"Well, I wasn't expecting you to stay and hang out. A goodbye would suffice though." He was irritated.

"You're right." I sighed. "I'm hung over and just want to get home. I could have been more courteous though." I hugged him and we said goodbye.

I rolled my eyes as I turned to leave his apartment and called myself a cab.

* * *

We spent the following week texting back and forth. We kept it light and humorous, I was intrigued by him. He was different and unapologetic. We clicked in a really unconventional way. He was smarter than

I initially gave him credit for. His reputation aside, he was actually quite a catch. I found out he was only bartending on the weekends. He had a day job running a family business, which explained the fabulous apartment. He was educated, humble and unpretentious. Most people had no idea about his double life. I asked him why he even worked in the bar industry. As a man with a career, I found it a strange choice. Most bartenders and servers are dying for a real job so they can escape their customer service hell. His response was that he worked at the strip club to save himself from spending too much money on the weekends.

This, ladies, is what you call a red flag. These are the words of someone with a severe party habit. Someone who is probably not boyfriend material, despite whatever the rest of the labeling on the package may read.

Late one Saturday night, I was trying to hail a cab after work when a limo pulled up beside me. I glared at the tinted window, assuming that inside the over-stretched sedan was a group of rowdy bridge-and-tunnel dickheads. I rolled my eyes as I could hear girls screaming over the loud music.

Suddenly the door swung open and Johnny's head popped out. He smiled before he reached for my arm and pulled me inside. I flopped onto him with a thud, in what was probably the most ungraceful limo entrance of all time. He slammed the door shut. "Okay, we're good Benny," he yelled to the driver as the car switched back into gear.

"What the hell is going on?" I laughed. The limo was packed with strippers and staff from the club.

"We're kidnapping you to come party with us," yelled one of the dancers as she handed me a bottle of blueberry flavored vodka. It wasn't whiskey, but this wasn't the time to be picky. Johnny watched me as I shrugged before taking a long swig. He laughed.

It was only a matter of seconds after we stumbled into Johnny's apartment before the strippers had made themselves at home. Some of them emptied drugs onto cheese plates and passed them around the party as others scoured the liquor cabinet. Johnny poured me a glass of whiskey and I watched as the girls steamrolled his entire living space. A couple of them stripped naked and started dancing on the coffee table as a group of doormen snorted lines off their giant implants. Girls were making out with one another between snorting more lines and swapping partners. I'd never seen anything like this. It was a sea of skin, silicon, cocaine, and daddy issues. I was a tourist, observing a shark feeding frenzy from a submarine. They were savages and I suddenly felt like a square peg being stuffed into a round hole.

After about an hour, Ginger, one of the dancers, approached me. In one hand, she was holding a cheese plate covered in orange and white powder, and in the other was an old Blockbuster card and a five-dollar bill. She held the cheese plate in front of me as she cut the two powders together with the Blockbuster card and formed two small lines out of them.

"Ever tried K?" she asked. Ginger was beautiful. She was older than the other girls and you could tell she mothered them, in a dysfunctional, anti-college kind of way. She'd been a feature dancer for 20 years and her experience offered an air of superiority and dominance. I looked into her glossy eyes, and watched her pouty, collagen-filled lips move as her words rolled off her tongue. "It's Ketamine, a horse tranquilizer. It's a downer. We mix it with uppers like coke and M. It sort of levels it out and gives you a better high. Want to try?"

This literally made no sense. Why even do drugs if the aim is to remain neutral? I hesitated. I'd dabbled in a little cocaine in the past but it wasn't my favorite. I'd definitely never done Ketamine. In fact, I didn't even know it was a drug that humans consumed. I shook my head. "Nah, I think I'm good, but thank you," I said politely.

"Oh, come on, how can you know you don't like it if you don't even try it, I promise it's safe." She pushed. This was starting to feel like that time Mickey convinced me his strep throat wasn't contagious.

"Talk about peer pressure," I joked as I snatched the rolled fiver out of her hand, leaned in and snorted the smaller of the two lines. It burned a little but overall it wasn't terrible. When the strippers' hen handler offers you a cheese plate covered in drugs, you snort them. This is how you gain their trust. They're like a top-heavy silicone mafia and once you snuff a guy, you're in. In this case, a guy is a horse tranquilizer. We ran out of drugs around the same time the sun came up. Funny how it always happens that way. Usually by then you should hate yourself enough to want to fall asleep anyways. So we did just that. I crashed in Johnny's bed for a few hours once everyone left.

It was a gorgeous fall afternoon when we woke up, so we decided to go for brunch. I squinted as we exited the building and reached into my purse for my sunglasses. I felt like a vampire, about to combust in the beating sun. We walked up the street side by side and Johnny reached for my hand. I looked up at him. The sun behind him casted a shadow over his face as he lightly squeezed my palm. We walked through the neighborhood and for the first time in a long time, I felt like maybe I was ready to date again.

* * *

Over the next few weeks we grew closer. We went on frequent dates: movies, concerts and dinners. I hadn't been wined and dined by a man since Billy. He took me to fancy restaurants, restaurants I probably couldn't afford on my own. I'll admit that it felt nice and it added to his charm. I arranged my weekend work schedule so that on Saturday nights I would be cut around 10 o'clock and could visit him at the club for a few drinks. We started spending a lot of time together. During the week, I would meet him for lunch or he would visit me at work. I quit smoking. Because I'd wanted to, but mostly because he thought it was gross.

When I found out that a band I really liked was playing a show in Seattle, I casually brought it up to him.

He didn't miss a beat, "Let's go!" he exclaimed.

"Seriously?" I asked.

"I love Seattle. Let's do it. I'll take care of transportation and the hotel if you get the tickets to the show." I jumped up with excitement. I'd never been to Seattle before.

We spent the drive swapping between our playlists and exchanging stories of travel and debauchery. We'd become friends. Before any sort of feelings, before the sex, before the chivalry, and before any expectations, we'd managed to build a really fantastic friendship. It confused people because there wasn't a label, but it didn't bother me. I knew I had his interest and for someone who was constantly surrounded by beautiful fuckbots, that felt like an accomplishment.

After the concert on the first night, we spent the weekend ordering room service, drinking in dives, shopping at record stores and vintage shops and eating terrible American food. We had an amazing couple of days together and when we returned home, rather than go our separate ways, we decided to order in and watch a movie at his place. Somehow, we hadn't grown sick of each other.

That night, after Johnny had fallen asleep, I got up to grab a glass of water. It was dark in the kitchen, but I was familiar with his apartment so I managed to navigate through it easily. As I was closing the fridge door, I saw his cell phone light up on the counter. Curious I leaned over to read the front screen. He had six missed messages from a Lisa. I felt a pang of interest and a part of me was begging to flip it open and browse. But I knew I couldn't go down that road again. I decided to blow it off and carefully made my way back into his bedroom.

* * *

A few weeks later, we were cleaning up his apartment after a night of partying. As I rummaged through the kitchen, putting clean dishes away, I noticed him across the living room, looking down as his phone and smiling. I flashed back to Lisa's name on his call display.

"Hey, I wanted to talk to you about something," I said, startling him.

He anxiously snapped his flip-phone shut, "Oh?"

I began to sweat. My communication skills have always been relatively subpar. I turn into *Rainman* the second I need to discuss anything that involves feelings. "I just. I just thought. What are we? I mean, is this moving forward, or?" I stumbled over my words as he was swept with nervousness.

"I don't know if I'm ready to have this conversation, honestly," he replied.

"Okay well I don't want to make this a thing. We just," I was struggling, "there's no label here and I want to know where I stand with you," I said in a direct tone, surprising myself.

He hesitated. "I told you I don't do labels, Jordan. We're having fun. I like you, but I'm not ready to be exclusive."

That hit me like a ton of bricks. This was not at all how I pictured this conversation unfolding. I stared at him blankly. I was hurt. I wanted to scream at him. I wanted to cry. I wanted to get the fuck out of his apartment. Without a single word, I grabbed my belongings off the counter and fled the scene.

When I finally stumbled outside, my breathing sped up. I leaned on the brick wall along the walkway and felt my heart attempt to heave straight through my chest and run away from me. I began to power walk toward my house. I had to get away from there. Away from him.

* * *

A week passed and I hadn't heard from him. I went about my life, uninterrupted. I missed talking to him, but not enough to sacrifice my self-respect. I assumed that was it, that it was over. Whatever *it* was. I'd started to like him too much to be another belt notch, so I knew I made the right choice.

One night, I was working behind the bar, getting ready to close up. My back was facing the door as I argued with a regular for payment when I heard someone bark a drink order from behind me. Irritated, I turned around to bite back. But there, smiling on the other side of the bar stood a very dapper Johnny. My body began to shake, as I was flooded with both anger and excitement.

"Surprised to see me?" He smirked.

I began to casually wipe off the beer taps, getting back to my business. "Look, I've already done last call, so you should probably go bother someone else with all your charm," I said sarcastically.

He smiled. "When are you done?"

"Probably not for another half hour. I'm managing tonight so I have to shut down," I said nervously.

"That's cool. I'll wait," he responded.

I looked up at him, stumped. "You'll what? I didn't say I wanted to hang out."

"I know. I'll just wait anyways, see what happens," he quipped.

I rolled my eyes. "Great, you can sit with Gary and convince him to pay me." I pointed to the drunk buffoon sitting behind me, who was now falling asleep. Johnny laughed.

We left the bar after I'd finished cashing out. The winter air was crisp. I pulled a toque over my head. "So, what did you have in mind?" I asked, looking for a cab.

"Well, I figure I owe you an explanation for last week and the Morrissey has an hour left before last call." he pointed to the bar across the street. I hesitated. I wasn't sure I was ready to have that conversation again. But I wondered what he had to say. I nodded and he grabbed my hand before we sprinted across the busy street.

We sat at the bar and ordered a couple drinks. Neither of us said a word at first. We just sat there, clumsily fidgeting with our glasses.

"So," he started. "I realize I was a bit of an asshole the other day. So, I'm sorry."

"Okay."

He looked at me curiously before he continued. "I like you. I really do. I find you interesting. You're smart and I only have a handful of smart women around. So, you've been an adjustment." He was extremely nervous and I could tell he didn't want to have this conversation at all. "With that said, my last breakup was really messy. So I'm really not ready for a girlfriend and I don't know when I'm going to be."

I took a deep breath. This wasn't exactly how I thought this conversation would go either, but he was being honest and for that I felt that he deserved my attention. "Uh huh, okay."

"You need to understand something about me, I'm turning thirty in the New Year and this is the first time that I've been single as an adult. I've bounced from relationship to relationship and clearly that hasn't worked for me. I'm not asking you to sympathize with me here, I just feel that you're someone who deserves an explanation." He was exasperated.

"Well, I guess that's fair. Thank you for your honesty. I'm struggling here because while I like you too and I value your friendship, I also want to be with you, so I don't really know where we go from here," I said.

"I know I would like to spend more time with you. But I want it to remain casual for now," he responded.

For now. Those despicable, compromising words, how dare men use them. But they do. And every single time it gives women hope. It's a faint light at the end of that dim tunnel. Women hang on to these words for dear life. It's pathetic and hopeless and we are aware of that. But every time we hear the words *for now* we melt into a puddle of *maybe* or even worse, *soon.* Ugh. If a man uses *for now* in reference to your relationship with him, spit into that fuckhead's drink and walk out the door. It's a trap.

Now, all this useful advice aside, I did what most women do anyways and I took a chance on *for now.* Because, well, I'm an idiot.

* * *

Weeks passed and Christmas began to rear its tacky, soul-sucking head. Johnny and I were right back where we left off before that awkward conversation in his living room. It was as if it never even happened. I wasn't sure if he was spending his spare time with anyone else, but he seemed interested in spending a lot of it with me so I tried not to think about it too much. I'd really started to care about him and I wanted him to want me back so I decided to play it cool. I decided to play the long game. Because as we've learned from history, allowing men to have their cake and eat it too will always eventually work to your advantage. (Said no intelligent person ever.)

My friendship with the strippers grew and so did my presence in that scene. I started getting Facebook friend requests from out-of-town strip club owners and agents. It's pretty safe to assume that a girl with big boobs and waist-length hair, who hangs out with a bunch of strippers, is probably also a stripper. The good news is that my mother finally stopped asking if I had turned gay. The bad news was that she was now convinced that I was rubbing up on strange dicks behind a velvet curtain to pay my rent.

One night, I was out with a friend from work when I received a text from Ginger about a friend's fundraiser at The Roxy. We were nearby having drinks at a local watering hole and decided it might be fun to pop by and say hi to everyone.

Upon entering the club, I spotted Johnny right away. He was hard to miss, the guy stood out like Michael Jackson at a child's birthday party. He was standing at the bar, chatting with a slender black woman. I pointed him out to my coworker as we made our way over to say hello. When he noticed me heading his way, he froze. His body language was off and as I approached him, I realized this woman wasn't a friend. But it was too late. I'd already passed the point of no return, pulling a tuck-and-roll was no longer an option. I shakily said hello as I approached them. The woman turned to face me and I almost jumped out of my skin in complete shock. She looked like a queen. In fact, *"does he know he's with a drag queen?"* was a legitimate thought that went through my head. I was confused and angry and completely unsure of what the fuck was going on. Picture Wesley Snipes in *Too Wong Foo*, minus the muscles. I just stood there. Staring at her. She was mesmerizing.

And then she caught me. She stared right through me. The glare from her dark eyes penetrated right through my skepticism and I couldn't look away.

"What's up, Jordan?" Johnny said coldly, interrupting the staring contest.

I shook my head as if to break the spell, and turned my gaze from her to him, and back to her, then rested on him. "I, uh, I saw you when I walked in and wanted to say hi. I. Uh." I couldn't find my thoughts, never mind my words. I was completely fazed by everything that was happening. How many ways did he swing? How did I miss this?

"Well, you've said hi. And made this extremely uncomfortable. So maybe you should go now," he responded.

Asshole Rating: 6.5 Dismissal is a dick move.

I snapped back into my uncomfortable reality. What did he just say to me? My entire body began to fill with rage. Was I being disrespected? In front of strangers? By a man in a wifebeater with whiskey stains down the front? Oh hell no. I couldn't ignore this. I very carefully calculated my next move. A) I wasn't sure if this was a woman or a man in ladies' shoes and B) if it was a man in ladies shoes, were they willing to hit a woman because they're dressed like one? I considered my imminent future as it flashed before me. My blood began to boil as my veins filled with steam. I glared at Johnny, burning a fiery hole through every inch of him. I could have set that idiot ablaze.

"What's your problem, bitch?" Noxeema Jackson piped in.

I turned my glare towards her and then back to him. I was so mad that I was on the verge of tears, when suddenly the unexplainable happened. I burst into compulsive laughter. I pointed at them and began to laugh harder. I tried to control myself. I couldn't. I just stood there laughing hysterically. I was being called out by a drag queen. At the Roxy. How apropos. This is what my life had come to. And I could not, for the life of me, stop laughing over it. I finally gathered myself enough to look at Johnny. He was extremely unimpressed. His date was one finger-wave from smashing me in the face.

"Are you finished?" Johnny challenged.

I composed myself long enough to answer, "Yes. I am. Wait, no, no, we are," I waved as I walked away from them, toward the front door. When I got to the door, I spun around and yelled, "Good luck with all that!" to her, before disappearing the same way I'd come in.

As my cab approached my apartment building, I burst into tears. I was confused and felt used. The Iranian driver looked at me in his rearview mirror, "Are you okay, Miss?" he asked, concerned.

I sobbed. "Yes. I'm sorry. What do I owe you?"

He watched me in the rearview as I cried. "You know, as a married man, may I offer you some advice?"

I looked up at his reflection in the rearview mirror, really hoping he'd save the pep talk for someone else. "I know, I'm a mess, I'm sorry."

"It's no worry at all but please believe me when I say that whoever is making you feel this way is not worth it. I see this too often. Childish men drive good women crazy every single day. Please take this ride as a gift and take care of yourself. Your money is no good here tonight." He smiled warmly.

I watched his reflection in the mirror and quickly began to realize how stupid I looked. I wiped my eyes and reached out, touching his shoulder. "Thank you. I'm sorry," I apologized again before I opened the door to get out. I closed the door behind me and waved as he sped off. Ugh. How embarrassing.

I fell asleep as soon as I hit my sheets, but I woke up only a couple hours later in distress. Hoping I'd received a text from Johnny, I leaned over to grab my phone off the nightstand. Nothing. I was still drunk. My eyes were the size of golf balls. Against all better judgment, I decided to text him. Only I didn't just send one solid, poignant text. I went off on a tangent. I'm talking full on, crazy-girl, power-text tangent. I ripped him apart and then waited a minute for a response. I knew he was with her, so when I didn't get a response, I sent another. And another. And another. Okay, honestly, I'm talking about this guy waking up to probably 36 mixed signals in a row. This was a low. I admit that. I fell asleep again, feeling good about what I'd said, over the span of 36 messages.

The next morning I woke up on the verge of suicide. What had I done? What was wrong with me? This was bad. And there was no recovering from it. There comes a time in every person's life when they realize the importance of the future invention of time machines. This was that moment for me.

Crazy Level: 5.9 Power-texting is only worth a higher rating if you're someone who uses emojis.

I would like to make something clear here. We were not in a relationship. I knew that. He had made this position very unequivocal. So, technically, dating other people was not inappropriate behavior. But I felt there was a certain responsibility to be mindful and respectful of each other's feelings. We were bound to run into one another. Vancouver is a small city and our circles comingled. His reaction was unfair and cruel on no more than a basic-friendship level.

He responded the following afternoon. His response was brief and to the point. He made no apologies for our run-in and basically told me that I was acting like a complete lunatic. Which, by definition, I was, but that didn't grant him a free pass to act like a selfish piece of shit. So, we were at a standstill. I never responded to that message. I figured I had probably sent enough messages to last a lifetime in the past 24 hours. I decided it was probably for the best that it ended right then and there.

* * *

Christmas was around the corner when I finally heard from him. He wanted me to meet him for lunch. I hovered over the invitation for nearly an hour before I gave in. Again. Like an abandoned puppy dog.

We met at a restaurant nearby. It was awkward and uncomfortable at first, but it didn't take long before I found myself flirting with him again. He told me about Wesley Snipes, the stripper from Alberta. Johnny had a thing for strippers in general, but black strippers specifically. He talked to me about her as though I were a buddy of his. It bothered me, don't get me wrong, but it was then I realized that I loved this person and for some confusing reason, I was willing to put up with his madness.

So began this weird, unintentional, open-relationship mess of a thing. No one understood it, least of all me, but I went with it. We did very couple-like things. I met his family and went to dinners with them. We spent holidays together. We slept in the same bed multiple times a week. It became a very bizarre fuck-buddy situation, but feelings were definitely running rampant. On the weekends, he would pick up girls at the bar and take them home, meanwhile I would get extremely jealous and turn it into a half-day fight, before all was forgiven and we were back on his couch watching wrestling and cooking dinner together. I taught myself to adapt to his lifestyle and I figured so long as I was getting angry at him when he was with other women, I was standing my ground. I'd become unhinged. I began partying all the time to numb the pain from the wreckage I'd gotten myself into. After all, God wouldn't have created cocaine if he didn't want us to self-medicate by forcing a stranger into repetitive conversations about the stupid business idea you have while snorting lines off their coffee table at 9 AM.

* * *

When he invited me to his parents' place in Mexico for a week, I was optimistic. I figured this would be a great opportunity to get some quality time with him. Maybe a trip together was what he needed to realize the error of his ways. Right, because the more time a man spends around a desperate woman, the more he'll want her.

At the very last minute, he invited Taylor to come along. Taylor was a family friend. She was personable, gorgeous, and a total trainwreck. I was annoyed he'd extended the invite, ruining our one-on-one time but there wasn't really much I could say about it.

On the night we were leaving, she'd gotten into a fight with her boyfriend and said she wasn't going to make it. I was relieved. But as my luck would have it, we were sitting on the plane waiting for the flight to finish boarding and suddenly she appeared behind the line of passengers. Taylor was completely disheveled, her makeup streaming down her face. Her hair was wet from the rain and she smelled like a nightclub carpet. But she'd made it. Unfortunately.

Our romantic vacation became a ridiculous over-the-top party. Taylor even decided to stay in our room. She slept on the couch most nights, but occasionally she stayed in the bed with us. We had weird, drunk threesomes and woke up the next morning with amnesia. It was a party-fueled, weeklong ménage à trois. Some nights we were all partying, having a great time and some nights Taylor was crying over her boyfriend back home and the shambles her life was in. It felt like we were traveling with every cast member from *Jersey Shore* rolled into one basket case.

One afternoon, we decided to head into the town. We wanted to do a little shopping and catch some lucha libre. This sounds like a joke. It's not. When we arrived at the wrestling stadium, Taylor began to have one of her meltdowns. We had been drinking all day and Johnny and I hadn't taken her low-tolerance into consideration. She turned into a wet noodle, suddenly obsessed with finding drugs. Apparently, she wanted to, in her words, "level out," so she began running around the stadium like a frantic moron looking for someone to sell her cocaine. We had to get her out of there before she got us arrested.

I'm not going to say I had a bad time. I was in Mexico, at a resort-like home, where the staff did my laundry and cooked our meals every day. I felt like Paris Hilton. I was grateful to him for bringing me, but of course it came with a price. That price, as usual, was my sanity.

* * *

So we carried on in our fucked-up whirlwind of weird sex, family dinners, strip clubs, gardening and cocaine. It was a strange time. Not one I'm completely proud of, but not one I would choose to erase from chalkboard either. I learned a lot of things. Mostly about patience and the extent to which I was willing to go to be made a fool. Like I said, it was a strange time.

We kept things casual, but that's not to say I didn't turn into a full-blown crackpot when I found out about other girls, because I certainly did. I started leaving my belongings around his condo in places I knew other girls would see them so they would realize they were on someone else's turf. I eventually insisted on having my own drawer in the night-stand next to the bed. If I found other girls' belongings lying around, I would throw them in the trash. I acted like a jealous psychopath. When I ran into him with other girls, I would make the situation so unbearably uncomfortable, that eventually they would leave wherever we were. I was a treat.

When I found out about a girl who was making frequent appearances at his place on the weekends, I decided to reel it in. I started to realize that changing him was going to be more difficult than I'd thought. So rather than take the high road and walk away with what little decorum I had left, I instead decided to stoop to his level. I wanted to make him jealous the way he made me jealous.

I started seeing someone new. Alex was a bartender and we knew each other through the downtown scene. I liked him. He was honest, he was handsome and he was great in bed. We would spend our time together drinking in dive bars, having sex while his dog watched, passing out and then waking up and stumbling to the greasy spoon up the street for brunch.

Johnny and I quickly and casually moved into friend-territory. One morning, after Johnny had begged for weeks to meet my mysterious new interest, I gave in. We decided to visit Alex at work.

We walked into the restaurant during a buzzing brunch and sat up at the bar. When Alex noticed me, he came out from behind the bar to give me a hug and I introduced him to Johnny. Alex was sweet and charismatic as he shook Johnny's hand. We made small talk before Alex had to get back to work. As he made his way back behind the bar, Johnny looked at me and without thinking before he spoke, he blurted, "How am I supposed to compete with that?" He was drunk, but it spoke volumes. A wave of satisfaction rolled over my conscience. It wasn't a competition, but if it was, I was winning.

I hung on to those words and over the following weeks I started to pull away from Alex as Johnny pulled me closer. He would invite me on small adventures with him, filling up my schedule so I didn't have any time left to spend with Alex. It was probably for the best though. Alex was a sweet guy and he deserved to be with a dog person who was unfazed by the irony of having sex doggystyle in front of a puggle.

Johnny and I had become entangled in a brilliant game of manipulation. I started to feel like things were finally headed in the right direction. I thought maybe he'd finally learned to appreciate what he had.

Don't worry, I was wrong. Again.

* * *

Summer rolled around, and all of our progress came to an unexpected pause when Bianca's stripper-hooker friend graced the city with her six-pack and perfect boob-gap. Bianca was a mutual friend that Johnny and I spent a lot of time partying with. She was constantly caught in the middle of our fights, but somehow always remained neutral. Her friend, the stripper-hooker, was a Vancouver girl who'd moved to

Australia and joined the nude circus. (Note: I'm not fully positive that she was also a hooker, but it's a safe assumption to make about strippers down under.)

As the obvious structure of storytelling would have it, Johnny fell hard for her. She was visiting for two weeks and he spent every free minute he had with her, leaving me in their dust. Clearly there was a theme here. I was jealous and obviously unhappy about it, but I'd hardened to his antics and knew she wouldn't be around for long. I stuck it out and kept myself busy until she left town. However, once she did leave, he was different. He wouldn't let her go. He would talk to her on the phone a few times a week. She would call on the nights we were spending time together and as soon as the phone rang, he'd jump up from whatever he was doing and run upstairs to talk to her. Sometimes he wouldn't return for an hour. I grew extremely jealous. And it certainly got worse when he asked her to meet him in Mexico for two weeks over Christmas.

Despite his new feelings for her, and my growing insanity, we remained close and I resumed my role as his makeshift girlfriend leading up to Christmas. As time crept by, he and the stripper-hooker grew apart. He eventually stopped talking to her almost altogether. When Christmas neared, he wanted to pull out of the plan. Things had gone stale between them and the excitement fizzled. But everything was paid for. He was financially bound to the trip.

The night before he left, Johnny broke down while we were watching TV. "I'm sorry," he said, cutting through the white noise.

"For what?" I asked.

"For always doing this to you. I don't know what my problem is. You deserve better."

"I've made my own choices. This situation isn't ideal and it kills me that you're taking her there. But honestly, we need time apart. I have to assess what I'm doing here," I responded. It came as a shock to both of us. He was taken aback and there was an uneasy silence that settled over us.

"You'll always be number one. You know that right?" I didn't know if that was supposed to be a compliment or an insult. The inner conflict became increasingly worse and further from a resolution. What the fuck does that even mean? How did I end up here in this torrid, evil string of control and misdirection? I'm beginning to think that I should have called this book *How Did I End Up Here?* Or *The Decent from Main Bitch to Side Bitch*.

He told me that she had decided to come back to Vancouver for a week after Mexico to see her friends and family and she had asked to stay at his place. This was the final straw. And by that, I mean it definitely wasn't the final straw.

He left the following morning. I knew I couldn't be there when they returned, so I booked a one-way flight to LA on the day I knew he would be flying home. I needed to reassess my life. I needed to get control of my future because this was heading nowhere fast.

He messaged me while he was in Mexico. All day, every day. He was miserable. He claimed the spark was gone and all he wanted to do was come home. I didn't feel sorry for him. When you take a hooker to Mexico, you might not have a fairytale ending. That's just the gamble you take.

* * *

My flight to LA took off about six minutes after their flight landed in Vancouver. I wasn't sure how long I wanted to stay, I just knew I needed to sort through the murky shit-filled-pond that my life had drowned in. I stayed with a mentor on Venice Beach. He was working on a writing project that he needed a little help with, so I decided to seize that opportunity as a chance to clear my head. I spent my afternoons alone, walking the boardwalk, taking photos, and writing on the beach until the sun went down. I was still messaging with Johnny every now and then but I did my best keep a clear conscience.

One afternoon while I was shopping, I received a text from Johnny. He was having a meltdown and begged me to come home. But I wasn't ready to go home, so I declined. Why was he doing this to me? I knew the stripper-hooker was still staying with him. Johnny was someone who needed constant adoration. If he wasn't getting the attention he needed from someone else, he would fall back on me. I'd become the ugly, wool Christmas socks you keep in the back of your drawer for nights when you're alone and the heater is broken. It wasn't his fault that I'd wound up here, it was my fault for allowing it. But he should have been man enough to let me go. Because we both knew he would never change.

I decided to fly home on my 25th birthday. I purchased the ticket the night before. I figured it was time to face reality. Well that, and I was broke. Johnny messaged me in the morning to say Happy Birthday. I was just about to board my plane so I thanked him and ended the conversation.

I made my way through YVR upon arrival. As the opaque door opened to the Arrivals room, I looked up from my phone and standing there at the end of the line was a very nervous Johnny. He was holding a bouquet of roses. A flood of mixed emotions swelled inside of me. I was angry, and happy, and sad, and confused all at the same time. I walked over to him and I stood there, just staring at him. I dropped my bags and reached up to hug him.

"Thank you for this," I whispered in his ear. It was one of those romance-movie grand gestures. He handed me the flowers and picked up my bag. He put his arm around me and we left the terminal.

When he pulled up outside of my apartment, he turned off the engine. "I want you to know that I kicked her out."

"Okay," I carefully responded, as I'd certainly heard this one before. "So where is she staying then?"

"Don't know. And don't care. She's an adult. She can sort her own shit out. Not my problem," he said casually.

"So that's it?" I questioned.

"That's definitely it. And I can't tell you how sorry I am. It was a mistake. A huge mistake," he said, nearly starting to tear.

"Okay so what now?"

"I don't know. I guess I should get back to work." He looked at me with a sort of sadness. Sadness that is only true to a guilt-filled man. And I looked at him with uncertainty. Uncertainty that is only true to a scorned woman.

"Do you want to come in for a birthday drink first?" I asked.

We made our way into my building and up the stairs to my apartment. I poured us a drink and put the flowers in a vase. I joined him on the couch. For a few minutes we just sat there, fiddling with the cushions and shifting uncomfortably. He finally reached over and pulled me closer to him. He started to sweat and his eyes glossed over. Something was up. He looked at me nervously, darting his stare from me to the photos on the wall and back to me.

"Are you okay?" I asked.

He stared at me. He began to shake and then suddenly he blurted, "I love you, Jordan."

Beat. Long, awkward beat. What. The. Fuck. I stared at him, confused, emotional, happy? I started to sweat too. I was in shock. I hadn't seen this coming.

"I. Are you sure?" I quizzed.

"I am."

I thought about his words. Long enough to frighten him. I thought about our situation. It wasn't ideal and it certainly wasn't promising but before I could think too hard about what was happening, I blurted, "I love you too." He smiled at me and hugged me. I think this is what it means to shake hands with the devil. At least I'm pretty sure.

* * *

Johnny's birthday came a week after mine. Things were good between us. I still wasn't sure if we were in a relationship, but it felt like we were. We hadn't discussed it, but we'd spent all of our free time together since I'd gotten back from LA. For the first time in a year and a half, it felt like all of my patience and persistence had paid off. But like most good things in life, it's only a matter of time before you're railroaded by some walking blow-up doll who only reads in order to find quotes to caption her selfies with. (That's probably not a quote I want to be remembered for.)

I showed up at his apartment on his birthday with a cactus. He laughed when he opened the door and I presented him with the strange gift.

"I guess I deserve that," he said as he took the cactus from me.

His mom was in the kitchen, making dinner. When she spotted me in the entrance, she walked over to give me a hug.

A few minutes later, his best friend showed up and the four of us sat down to dinner. Johnny looked around the table and smiled. "I'm surrounded by my three favorite women, I'll cheers to that," he said, raising his glass. We all clinked our glasses in unison.

After dinner, Johnny and I decided to go out and tour the city. We bounced around from bar, to strip club, to bar, visiting friends along the way. And before heading home, we popped into the Roxy for last call. We met up at the back bar with a couple friends and a few minutes later Johnny handed me his drink as he excused himself to use the bathroom.

Time passed. A lot of time. He still hadn't returned after twenty minutes. Curious where he'd wound up, I went looking for him. I paced around the bar, through the crowd but I couldn't find him anywhere. He'd completely disappeared. Just as I was about to give up, I spotted him at the back of the u-shaped bar near the entrance of the club. He was talking to a shorthaired girl. I was about to walk over to them but I stopped myself when I saw him put his hand on the small of her back. Curious, I decided to stand back and watch. I didn't want to overreact if she was just a friend. Then, exactly as expected, he leaned over and kissed her. The kiss lasted forever. People around them were starting to get uncomfortable. I began to see red. I couldn't control myself. The erratic spaz erupted like a merciless volcano near a third world village. As he pulled away from her, I sped towards him. I was manic. Possessed. Something had taken over and I couldn't contain it. As I approached him, I reached up and threw my fist into the side of his head. He flung back and grabbed his temple as he looked at me. I was no longer myself. I'd become a crazy little demon version of myself. He knew he'd been caught and just stared at me, unsure what to do. The girl started swearing at me. I ignored her as I continued to glare at him.

"What the fuck is wrong with you? Happy birthday, asshole." With that, I spun around and stormed out of the club. I hopped into one of the cabs waiting outside and went home.

Crazy Level: 9.3 Violence is only the answer when the question is: How can I make myself the least desirable?

I received a text from him the following morning, basically telling me that I owed him an apology and when I had one for him, he would be willing to hear it. I didn't respond. I felt no apology was owed. When you reach a point of delusion where you feel it's acceptable to hit people because of the way you allow them to make you feel, it's time to get a therapist, or at the very least, an Ativan.

After I didn't hear from him for a week, I started to feel sad and alone. I eventually broke down and messaged him: *"Can we talk?"*

He responded immediately: *"I don't have anything to say to you if you don't have an apology for your behavior."*

I told him I wanted to talk in person and asked if he would meet me for lunch. He agreed. Like he always did. I never did apologize. Instead, we found a way to sweep it under the rug as usual. It seemed as though neither of us really had any standards when it came to one another. We were just incapable of letting each other go.

On it went. Johnny was back to his old tricks and I was back to my old misery. It was as if the conversation on my birthday hadn't even happened. Girls came and girls went. And with each one came a fight, followed by forgiveness. I started to realize that I was in a world of shit. The deeper I went, the more I loved him and the harder it became to stand up for myself. I was depressed and stopped caring about my actions. I would do obsessive things like call and text him over and over again when I knew he was with someone else. One time I noticed a third toothbrush in the holder of his ensuite bathroom. I picked up the toothbrush and scrubbed the inside of the toilet with it and then set it back in the holder. I became vile and vindictive as I slowly felt myself going insane. My jealousy had become a cancer. I was catty and painful to be around. I'd become someone you avoided at parties, which is maybe the only thing that's worse than being a movie extra.

In the spring, I decided it was time for a change. I was offered a bartending job at a new restaurant that had just opened. I took the job. I needed the fresh air of new employment.

On my first night, I walked up to the bar to introduce myself to the other bartender. He had his back turned to me as he wiped the counter and mingled with a regular. I tapped him on the shoulder and when he spun around I think I might have actually gasped for air. "I'm Malcolm. You must be Jordan," he said, smiling. This man was beyond beautiful. He was like the male model that you see in one of those stupid emails your mom forwards you. You know the ones that tell a corny, sexually-charged housewife joke, and then when you scroll to the bottom, there's a photo of some sex-on-a-stick, dressed in the male-stripper version of a blue-collar uniform. That was Malcolm. He looked me up and down, almost surgically. I knew this was going to be trouble. We both did.

We flirted every minute we spent behind that bar, to a point where our coworkers made assumptions that we were sleeping together. While it was a fair assumption to make, we kept it soft. At first. But I started to feel alive again. I had something to look forward to. Something Johnny wouldn't be able to take away from me. I began to spend more time with my new coworkers. I enjoyed going to work. It became an escape from the traveling freak show I'd made of my life. A life that seemed to be spiraling at a rapid pace.

One night after work, a group of us wound up in a game of poker at our manager's apartment. It was during the Canucks/Bruins playoff series, so it had been insanely busy at the bar and we all needed to unwind. During the poker game, Malcolm rested his hand on my leg under the table. There was so much pent-up sexual tension between us that his touch made me jump. I nervously excused myself from the group to refill my drink. Malcolm followed me into the kitchen. I felt his presence behind me as I was pouring the whiskey. When I finished, I set the bottle back on the counter and before I had an opportunity to pick up the glass, he spun me around and kissed me.

Suddenly a voice boomed from the living room, "Jordan, bring the Jack in here, will you? I need another drink." Startled, we jumped back and nervously stared at each other.

"Want to get out of here?" He asked.

I nodded.

"Okay," he said. "I'll leave first. Wait ten minutes and meet me outside."

I agreed. I picked the bottle of whiskey up off the counter and made my way back into the dining room. I don't think we were fooling anyone when I left shortly after him, but the idea of a work tryst was what made it so exciting.

When I exited the building, Malcolm was standing under the large overhang outside the door. The light rain had turned into a torrential downpour. He looked at me with a mischievous smile. "I only live two blocks away. Make a run for it?" I smiled back at him. He reached for my hand and we took off, sprinting through the rain.

We were soaking wet and panting by the time we made it to his front door. As we entered his apartment, I took off my jacket. The rain had soaked through both my coat and the white t-shirt I had on underneath it, exposing my bra. He walked over and lifted my shirt over my head. My nervousness made him laugh before he walked away and hung the wet t-shirt over a chair. Then he disappeared into the bedroom. When he returned, he was shirtless, holding a plaid button-up in his hand. He handed the shirt over to me.

"Thank you," I said as I quickly crawled into it and fastened a couple of the buttons.

"Can I get you something to drink?"

"Sure. What do you have?" I replied as he headed into the kitchen.

"Gin or Vodka," he called.

I looked around his apartment. "Vodka," I called back. "With a little water." There were boxes and moving bins everywhere. A few pieces of art were stacked against the wall, but nothing was hung. "Did you just move in or something?"

"Sort of," he said as he walked into the living room, holding a drink in each hand. He passed me a glass. "My uncle passed away a little while ago so when his house sold, I was left with the contents of the estate. This is all the stuff I've decided to keep."

"Wow, I'm really sorry," I replied.

"It's okay. We were prepared for it," he said, taking a sip of his drink.

We sat on the couch, attempting to get to know one another without immediately jumping all over each other. Malcolm was interesting. He was well-travelled, well-read and he had a body you could poach an egg on. Wait, that can't be right.

I lifted my drink to take a sip and realized it was empty. He snatched the glass out of my hand and set it on the coffee table. He stood up from the couch and reached out to help me up. He led me into his bedroom. I sat on his bed as he lit candles and turned some music on. I realize how incredibly cheesy this sounds and it certainly was, but it wasn't awkward. He was a pro. His sexual energy was so intense that he could have lit incense, applied lipstick, and then put on a jacket he made out of human skin before tucking his dick between his thighs, and I wouldn't have flinched.

He took my clothes off and started kissing my chest, then my stomach, hips and thighs. Before long, we were naked and covered in sweat, listening to Third Eye fucking Blind as we spawned a cliché dalliance.

Malcolm was the best sex I'd had (with another human) in a long time. His passion was the type of thing you would get lost in and not care to ever return from. He was an escape. Johnny and I didn't have bad sex. But there was so much resentment and animosity by this point that it was impossible not to wonder how many foreign snail-trails we were rolling around in every time we had sex. So, I guess there were distractions.

I grew an addiction to Malcolm, and okay, his ability to inflict multiple orgasms probably had something to do with it. But there was a hitch. He was an actor. Cringe. Actors are the most irritating people to date. They're vain, they take themselves way too seriously and they don't know how to shut the fuck up when you're watching a movie. I don't need to hear about the actor's troubled childhood or what type of lighting it took to create the scene, and I definitely don't want to listen to you quote the entire film, scene for scene. Be quiet and enjoy the cinematic experience, you know-it-all tit. This isn't a casting couch.

We decided it was best to keep it a secret. If anyone asked, we denied it. I'd been wrapped up with a coworker in the past, let's not forget bro-life Dale, so I knew the dangers of growing an attachment in the workplace. We agreed to keep it on strict friends with benefits terms. Johnny grew curious when I was no longer available at his convenience. He would message me to meet with him after work almost every night. I would lie and tell him that I was working late when really, I was on my way to Malcolm's house.

One night he decided to drop by the bar unannounced. I was working with Malcolm when he pulled up a stool and ordered a drink. I introduced them. Malcolm was polite and Johnny didn't think anything of it.

At one point, I reached over the bar to grab a stack of empty glasses. As Malcolm swept behind me, he casually, but intentionally, grazed my ass. I think he thought he was being discreet, but when I glanced up in Johnny's direction and saw the look on his face, I knew that wasn't the case. And honestly, I didn't care. Compared to the amount of his bullshit I was inundated with on a regular basis, this was child's play. I was single and I could sleep with whomever I pleased. Johnny paid his bill and left.

I received a text from him a couple hours later: *"Should have figured something was up. I won't be coming by there again. Have fun with your new 'friend'."*

That condescending motherfucker. Quotations? Really?

I didn't respond. Instead, I went home with my new *"friend"* that night and let him *"fun"* me into next week.

Once Johnny realized I had no remorse and wasn't interested in entertaining his behavior, he began to ask questions. He was jealous, really jealous.

Johnny asked me to meet him for lunch one afternoon. I wasn't doing anything so I agreed to meet him at the restaurant below his office.

When I arrived, he immediately started in on Malcolm. Something came over me as I watched him fret over my extracurricular activity. It was an overwhelming urge to be cruel, an urge that I hadn't felt before.

"Don't keep asking questions you don't want answers to," I said, repeating the sentence he'd used on me in the past.

"What is that supposed to mean?" he replied.

"I'm just saying, asking about my sex life with someone else, is probably not really going to end well."

"I don't care if you're having sex with someone else. I just don't understand why you would lie to me about it," he asked.

"You're the one who says your relationships with other people aren't my business, why is it different for you?" I snapped.

"Because you're catty about it," he responded.

"Oh, I suppose you're genuinely interested then?"

"Well, I just thought we were supposed to be honest with each other," he said.

"Okay, why don't you start us off."

"I don't tell you things for your own good, Jordan," he patronized. He was starting to piss me off and I wasn't in the mood for it. All I wanted was to eat a decent sandwich I wouldn't have to complain about and to enjoy a few glasses of mediocre wine. Why was he sabotaging a perfectly average afternoon?

And then it just sort of sputtered out of me, like sparks from a dying fire. "Okay, fine. Malcolm is the best sex I've ever had. Is that what you want to hear? I lie to you about going to his house because I'm thrilled about having multiple orgasms and don't want you to ruin that for me." I sat back and stared at my lunch.

He looked at me in silence. I had won this round. He was defeated and disappointed. I didn't care. Everything was a game with Johnny. I still loved him. If he told me then and there that he wanted to be with me, I probably would have quit my job and never spoken to Malcolm again. But he didn't know that. Instead, he was left feeling the same way he'd made me feel for the past two and a half years. And if I couldn't have him, well I guess his misery would do.

Manipulation is a funny thing. While men spent all those centuries oppressing women, women were secretly learning how to manipulate men.

After about six months, Malcolm and I pulled the plug. We drifted apart. He started seeing someone new and Johnny had become more persistent again. We continued to work together and remained friends just like we had planned. It was probably for the best. He could go back to decorating his apartment and I could go back to watching movies in peace.

* * *

Johnny and I shifted back in each other's direction, as we always did when we were lonely and feeling particularly pitiful. We planned a trip to Hawaii with his best friend and her fiancé. And, I mean, it was a great trip, despite the afternoon I busted him texting one of his floozies. I say that like I wasn't one because it puts me more at peace with my insecurity.

Johnny was unable to be in the moment. He was someone who always needed to remain connected with whatever was going on in whatever party scene he wasn't currently immersed in. He needed constant coddling from multiple angles. I'm not making excuses for him. I could have murdered him, but this is just who he was. And it's because of this that I always felt like I wasn't good enough. I always felt like I had to prove something to him and once I figured out what that was, and accomplished it, he would change his mind and move the bar up a notch. It was a very long, exasperating game of cat and mouse. A game I wouldn't be able to win because the real issue here was that he just wasn't in love with me the way I was in love with him. When a man loves you, he will do whatever it takes to be with you, not throw you into an empty well without a ladder.

This shouldn't come as much of a surprise, but it wasn't long before Johnny met someone who piqued his interest again. And she wasn't even a stripper. She was a young, naïve, gorgeous little thing with a lust for pseudo vampires, Jared Leto, emo memes, and then of course, Tumblr: the emotional diarrhea dumpster.

When Johnny's friend introduced them, he fell all over himself for her. But there was a minor glitch; Vivian was technically a lesbian. A lesbian who would engage in heterosexual flings. Whatever that meant.

Their affair made me extremely green-eyed. But I knew she was fleeting, just like the rest so I did my best to stay out of it while remaining idle. Okay, if I haven't stressed this enough, I was clearly delusional.

Where was my backbone? My integrity? I had completely lost my mind. Johnny and I still saw each other but Vivian consumed a lot of his time. They were on and off. Maybe because she was young and flippant, maybe because she had a hard time getting past the whole penis thing, who knows?

Johnny managed to wrangle last-minute box seat tickets to the Chili Peppers show one afternoon. He knew I had an affinity for Anthony Keidis so he didn't even bother to ask me if I wanted to go, he just told me to be ready by seven. At this point, he and Vivian were off but coasting in friend territory. I was happy she was finally out of the picture and back to her scissoring ways.

When the stadium lights went out and the show was about to start, Johnny pulled a capsule of MDMA from his pocket. He sprinkled half of the white powder into my drink and the other half into his own.

In minutes, we were coasting on a cloud of bold dance moves and unnaturally ginormous smiles that reached around our heads. That show will probably go down in history as the most fun I've ever had at a concert. And if not, it will go down as the most I've ever suggestively touched random strangers at one.

After the show, we wound up at a little bar in Gastown. Johnny showed me a text from Vivian asking him to meet her not long after we arrived. "Tell her to come down!" I shouted over the music, high out of my mind.

"Are you sure you want to meet her?" he asked.

"Oh hell, why not?" I yelled as I continued to dance. Awkwardly. By myself.

Vivian showed up about 15 minutes later. She was shy and bumbling as she hid behind her huge mane of long, curly, black hair. She was fair-skinned (for a mixed girl) with huge eyes and a tiny frame. She looked better in real life than she did in photos. Something I didn't think was even possible. And I was so high that I couldn't even be jealous. I introduced myself to her right away and then pulled her into the women's washroom with me to feed her some MDMA.

Before long, we were all high, rolling around naked in Johnny's bed. Don't ever let anyone tell you that your bad dance moves will stop you from getting laid, because I'm a living testament that that is just simply not true. Johnny and I had experienced a few threesomes together by this point but this was one of the better ones. Vivian was a lesbian, after all. I was attracted to her and I understood why he was too. In fact, you would have to be a Catholic priest not to be attracted to this woman.

Viv and I sparked up a friendship with Johnny's encouragement. We caught movies together and met over drinks. We would chat about all sorts of things. Or, well, I would chat and she would listen. She was younger than me with significantly less life experience so she found some kind of mentoring wisdom in my companionship. She always seemed in awe, which contrasted her enigma.

One afternoon Ginger called me with three passes to the Marilyn Manson show that night. We mentioned it to Johnny but he wasn't interested. He told us to invite Vivian because she was dying to go to the show.

The three of us wound up partying on the tour bus after the show. There I was stuck between a Barbie doll stripper and a half-black pseudo lesbian, staring at Marilyn Manson's smudged guyliner, go figure. The band was sober because I guess they were setting out to achieve the most boring tour bus experience of all time, so we did what any good asshole would do in this situation, we sat around cracking sobriety jokes and making everyone uncomfortable. Once they ran out of booze, and we ran out of patience, we decided to ditch the party and retreat somewhere with even more cum stains on the furniture: The Roxy.

Ginger wound up leaving the bar with some local restaurant magnate after blowing him in the bathroom, so there I was with Viv, waiting for a cab at closing time. Suddenly without much hesitation, she asked if she could stay at my place. This was new, and exciting, and I was wasted so I probably would have said yes to almost anything.

When I woke up the next morning, I was naked and Vivian was gone. She left an apologetic note on the table in the front entrance. She signed Viv with a heart above the i.

Johnny messaged me in a panic later that morning. Apparently, he was unable to get ahold of Vivian all night and was worried something happened to her. I found his concern for her offensive. I told him she was fine and not to worry about it.

I wasn't interested in a relationship with Vivian (obviously) and I started to distance myself from Johnny. His obsession with her became distressing and annoying. And I mean, I had my own shit to sort through. I was clearly battling a What-if-I'm-a-lesbian-now-how-do-I-tell-my-grandparents? problem.

Viv and Johnny eventually had a blowout. By this time, I really didn't care to help him through it. I was done being his therapist and his backup plan. So instead of entertaining Johnny's problems, I did what all crazy girls do when loneliness becomes a fixture, I got a cat.

He asked me to meet him for lunch one afternoon. I agreed and we met at a quaint restaurant close to my house. When I approached him, he looked sad but he quickly mustered a smile.

I gave him a hug. "How are you?"

"I'm okay. How's the new kitten?"

"Adorable."

After we ordered lunch, he turned to me, "I'm going to Mexico again next week. We are chartering a private plane. Why don't you come? It'll only be for a few days."

"I don't know." I hesitated.

"As friends. You can have your own room and everything. I just know you're easy to travel with."

I thought about it. Flying private sounded exciting and his dad's place was an absolute sanctuary. "Okay, let me see if I can get my shifts covered," I said. I made a few calls and rearranged my work schedule so I could get away for five days.

We spent the first three days soaking up the sun, laughing, sleeping in separate rooms and getting along. Which was an accomplishment, honestly. Maybe we could be friends. Maybe we'd made the most difficult transition of all time?

Nope. But wasn't that a cute thought?

One evening after dinner, he came into my room. I had just gotten out of the shower so I was flicking through channels in my robe. We watched a few minutes of garbage TV before he reached inside my robe. We lunged at each other. We hadn't been together in over two months and in that moment, we turned animalistic.

The next day, as we wandered around the local market, we held hands. And for a moment, we experienced that magnetic pull, the same charge we felt three years prior, before all the games and the bullshit. For the first time in a very long time, we looked at one another like we actually enjoyed each other.

But it was only for a moment.

He was glued to his phone the entire ride back to the house. When we pulled into the driveway, I finally built up the courage to ask what was so important. He shrugged it off.

But I pushed further. "It's Vivian isn't it?"

He was guilty but hardly upset about it. "Yes," he responded.

I turned ice cold. He tried to console me but I wasn't interested. We would never work out and it was finally clicking for me. I would never change him. No matter what I tried to sell, he wasn't buying.

We left Mexico the following morning and then went our separate ways.

* * *

A couple weeks before Christmas, Johnny messaged me to meet him for a few drinks. He wanted to bury the hatchet. And according to the Mayans it was the night before the end of the world. Everyone knows you're basically obligated to hold out an olive branch if the world is ending.

We swilled whiskey as we bounced around the local strip clubs. By the time it was last call, we were obliterated and he invited me over to his place for a nightcap.

When we arrived, he poured a few drinks as I sat on the counter in his kitchen. We exchanged stories about the past couple weeks. We were friendly and it felt warm. I finally felt like I didn't want him anymore. Until his phone began to light up.

"Who is that?" I asked.

"It's Alison. I told her she could come over tonight. Is that okay?"

I guess I began to fume. Alison was another girl on his rotation. We were having such a great evening. Why did he always have to do this?

"You're kidding me, right?" I responded. "Why would you put me in this position? Obviously I don't want to hang out with some girl you want to fuck. What's wrong with you?"

He laughed. Which is a really great way to calm down a crazy person. "As if you care. You're welcome to leave if it's that big of a problem." He looked at his phone and continued to text before he glanced up at me. "She's on her way, just so you know. If you don't want to be here, I suggest you leave."

I can't really remember what happened next, but I know I saw red. For the second time. Murderous red. The fury took over as I snapped myself off the counter and surged toward him. I began to shriek and roar. The pressure that was building up over the previous three years had totally collapsed the floodgate. I screamed at him an inch from his face, in a full-on rage, evicting all of it like an unwanted tenant. Until I had nothing left to say.

I stood there, my face still only an inch from his. There wasn't anything left to yell but I was still so angry. So, I pushed him away from me. He stumbled back a step before he reached out with a cupped open-palm, and slapped me in the face. I froze. He froze. And we just looked at each other in horror.

Asshole Rating: 9.3 Because slapping a woman is only okay when you're balls deep in romantic lovemaking.

I reached up to place my palm on my cheek and felt the warmth of his hatred.

"Get out of here, you psycho," he yelled.

I stumbled backward, toward the front door. He moved closer to me as I fumbled to put my boots on. I stood up, about to leave, when he suddenly fumbled forward and crashed into me. I fell to the floor. He was hammered and unaware of his own weight. I stood up and grabbed my coat, before I ran out of the apartment.

I spastically pressed the button for the elevator. Once the doors opened and I stepped inside, I repeatedly hit the Close Door button. The doors finally began to move as I watched Johnny barrel out of his apartment. But before he could reach the capsule, it sealed shut and slowly dropped down the shaft.

I exited the lobby and ran out onto the street. I saw a cab turn the corner up the road just as Johnny came running out of the building, "Jordan, I'm sorry! I shouldn't have done that! Please stop!" he yelled.

"Get the fuck away from me!" I screamed back as the cab pulled up. I jumped inside and gave the cabbie my address before we sped off.

The driver watched me in the rearview mirror as we neared my destination. Finally, he asked, "Everything okay? Should you call the police?"

"Everything is fine. Just take me home please," I responded.

This was a colossal fuck up. Who had we become? And what did we stand for? This torrid love affair had turned both of us into monsters. He wanted me to be there, but he wouldn't let me have him the way I wanted. It was a dead end, no matter which way you looked at it. We'd grown to hate ourselves so badly that we were willing to drown each other as we scrambled to fight over a life preserver that could have easily saved us both.

That was the last time I spoke with Johnny.

* * *

When you take a step back and think about all the loves you've had and the loves you've lost, one thing generally rings true: none of them were ever worth the sacrifices you made. We do things we aren't proud of as we dangle ourselves like bait on a very thin wire. And whether that thin wire represents honesty, fragility, vulnerability, or innocence, we are all hopelessly fighting for the same, unattainable thing: desirability. But desire becomes a mirage as you desperately stumble through a desert unwilling to compromise for unclean water. And once you're on the brink of death, that unclean water, while abhorrent and likely swimming with parasites, is the only thing that can keep you alive. So you embrace it as its murkiness surges through your body, and suddenly all your thirst disappears. Like it never even existed in the first place.

Johnny and I finally bridged the divide after three and a half years. Now we have the friendship we owed each other from the start. Well, until he reads this book.

But you know, it was probably for the best. I can be a lot of things, but I'll never be a black stripper.

CHAPTER 6.5:
PERSISTENCE

"Everybody is not a victim"

—Bill Cosby, (Alleged) Rapist

I spent three long years playing a victim. I wouldn't accept the reality of the situation and I couldn't wrap my head around why the Playboy didn't want to be with me, so I acted out. I did stupid, manipulative things to get his attention. When it backfired and I was left looking like a lunatic, I would justify my actions by convincing myself, and everyone around me, that my actions were a product of his mental abuse, that whatever he did was worse. I was a mess and I blamed him for stringing me along.

The Playboy was desperate for company and attention, so whenever he wasn't getting it from a stripper he would default onto me. He did cruel and heartless things, things that wound up separating me from my identity. I felt used and embroiled in a world of shit. It was a complete mind game. Start to finish. We loved each other but we loved to hate each other more. Every time I began to pull away, he would cast the line to reel me back in and I would start to see that faint light at the end of the proverbial tunnel. The Playboy was a textbook asshole. And I had become textbook crazy.

But I had a choice. I chose to stay and remain complicit. I chose to bite down on the hook. The only person I was victimized by was, well, me. I was the biggest asshole of all, dragging my friends and family through the bipolar chaos I'd made of my life. I spent an equal amount of time turning him into the Boogieman as I spent praising him. I constructed scenarios and problems where there really weren't any because truth of the matter was he just wasn't that into me. Sure, he loved me. We were best friends. He loved me the way I love my cat. But there was never a future for us. I didn't intrigue him enough. I'm okay with it now, but I'd be a complete liar if I said it wasn't one of the worst blows to the ego that I've ever endured.

I've spent hours, days, months even, trying to mathematically solve our equation. Once it ended, I became determined to make sense of what happened. Where we went wrong and how we let it get so out of control. I couldn't understand why he treated me the way he did or why I let him. Even more so, I couldn't understand what was wrong with me, why I wasn't good enough for him. I eventually realized that it wasn't me at all. No one was good enough for him because the Playboy wasn't good enough for himself. He wasn't a happy man and I certainly wouldn't have been the right person to turn him into one. Men like the Playboy need a comfort blanket. Someone to rub their hair at the end of the day and assure them that the world isn't going to shit, that they're not just a part of the downstream flow and that tomorrow might be the day that world hunger is resolved.

I am not that person. I'm cold and independent. He needed someone warm, someone who needed him, someone who would dote on him despite his array of idiosyncrasies and awkward social habits. That's just not who I am. I'm a brute. I call people on their madness. I'm abrasive, cynical, and spiteful. I'm basically an 80-year-old curmudgeon with really great hair.

The Playboy had a thing for crazy girls, so I went to the depths of my own insanity just to try to reach him. But his inability to love me the way I wanted him to, drove me off the rails. It certainly didn't stop me though. The chase was like a drug. The worse he treated me, the more I wanted to change him. In turn, he put up with a lot of shit. I became a soundtrack of stupidity. I'm still working to gain back the intelligence I lost in those three years. I'm not proud of the things I did or the things I said. I was about one episode at the Roxy away from setting his Cadillac ablaze with him inside of it. I turned into someone I hated. Again. I had roofed the ball. It was a real Randy Quaid moment for me.

But instead of racing off into the sunset on my crazy carpet, I bought a Persian cat and channeled all of my insanity into my inner cat-lady. I like to think I got out just in time. The Playboy made me crazier than my previous experiences had left me and I couldn't turn it off. Which definitely turned *him* off.

That said, I worry he turned me into someone who's hard to love.

* * *

Take someone like Linda Riss who dumped her boyfriend, Burt Pugach, when she found out he was married. This seems like the logical and sane approach to that sort of a problem. Anyways, Linda moves on to someone new and presumably Burt carries on with his marriage. Wrong. Burt wasn't having it. He wanted to have his cake and eat it too, so when Linda rejects him, the unspeakable happens.

This poor woman is blinded and mutilated when a hit man, hired by Burt, shows up at her front door one casual afternoon with a handful of lye. She suffered third degree burns to her eyes and face because some asshole was angry that she wouldn't be his side ho.

Linda was engaged to her new beau at the time of the attack and then that asshole calls off the wedding because now she looks like Rocky Dennis.

This gets better.

Burt winds up doing 14 years in prison for the crime. Once he's released, he divorces his wife and continues to vie for Linda's love. Meanwhile, she's blind and can't get a date to save her life, so she does what any other self-respecting woman does, she forgives Burt for blinding her and welcomes him back. They get married and live crazily ever after.

What in the actual fuck happened here?

Burt turned Linda into a goddamn mutant so that no one else would want her, in hopes that eventually he would win her back. I mean,

I guess that's one way to weed out the competition. If you're Tonya Harding. But the worst part of this story isn't that he maimed the woman he loved. The worst, and certainly the most confusing, part is that it totally worked! Linda was so desperate for companionship that she ran back into the arms of the same person who made her impossible to love.

Take a minute to let that sink in.

I'll wait.

What the hell is wrong with the human race? Where did we go wrong? Where in time did this glitch occur that made us so unbelievably pathetic? Is science currently working on the ability to travel through time and fix this problem? I mean they must be, right?

Linda and Burt Pugach land on the polar opposite end of my theory with the most divine, yet extreme analogy. Linda was a nice girl who, before Burt, sat at a comfortable low-medium crazy. Burt was a cheater, rendering his degree of asshole higher than Linda's degree of crazy. They meet, which pushes her out of the low range and deep into the medium range. Burt then soars from moderate asshole to Supreme King of Asshole County by committing the unforgiveable. The unforgivable then launches Linda past the cuckoo's nest, which is where she had to go to find forgiveness for the unforgivable.

If my crazy/asshole theory were bottled up and sold in weird Asian black markets, Linda and Burt would be on the warning label. Burt was such a ginormous asshole that he pushed Linda to utter insanity, which ultimately gave them room to unify. Oh, the irony of it all. There was never hope for Linda and she never even realized it. It's probably the saddest happy ending of all time.

* * *

I didn't learn a lot about relationships from my experience with the Playboy. What I did learn, aside from how to mix the perfect upper-downer cocktail, was the extent of my emotional elastic. I learned that given the right recipe for disaster, that elastic will snap and that I'm no hero. I will lose control of my emotions and cause nothing but severe embarrassment for everyone, most of all myself. I learned that searching for insanity to achieve the attention of someone you desire isn't a safe gamble to make because you may never come back from it. And you certainly can't blame your lunacy on the actions of someone who's just trying live their life banging strippers. It's really not fair to the strippers.

EPILOGUE

(Otherwise known as that thing you probably won't read, but should)

"My book has a very simple surface, but there are layers of irony and paradox all the way through it."

—~~Mark Haddon~~ Me

I guess I always thought I was special, that no matter what happened, I would always be able to remain in control of myself. After Billy, I assumed I'd gone through the worst of it. That I would choose better the next time. And then again the time after that. And after that. I was convinced that I would always continue to evolve, rather than deteriorate. I certainly never expected to come completely unhinged. But I'm not special and I don't obtain superior genetic makeup that grants me the power of veto to Crazyland. I don't even have advice on how to avoid it. All I have are my stories, my cynicism, and an ability to laugh at my misfortune.

I chose poorly. I chose companions who continuously made me crazier than I already was. And just when I would think I'd regained a grip on my sanity, another asshole, worse than the last, would come along and knock me off my feet.

Ultimately, my sights just weren't adjusted. They were set on some ridiculous idea that I could fix them, that I was able to readjust their asshole setting to match my level of crazy. This is a sickness, one that I hope researchers eventually find the cure for.

The amount of bullshit humans will take and how quickly they'll get up only to fall back down again is nothing short of fascinating. Masochists, all of us. We're a soulless, confused race of certified idiots, impervious to the elements as we run around inside this fucked-up utopia that society has fashioned out of marshmallows, convincing us that our bubble-wrapped dramas are important, that we are important.

We reject people and things that are good for us, because we want more. We want that drama, that passion, that excitement. We want that magical, movieland love that we assume is ubiquitous and free. We want to live up to the ideals of our idols because we only live once, right? So when we find something we like, we try to conform it to fit inside the frame of these delirious expectations. But people aren't things that can be remodeled into something that better suits your experience. You can't change people and you shouldn't even try. The best you can do is learn to choose more wisely. You cannot force someone to love you, that's like trying to light a cigarette in the wind. Find a life within your means. And find a love within the borders of reality.

We all come into this world confused and cold as hell. And eventually we all leave it the same way. The experiences we encounter as we push on waiting for the sweet release of death are what make us unique from one another. The key to finding happiness through those experiences—write this down—is to not be such a cunt all the time. Not everything is about you. In fact, nothing is ever really about anyone. When life deals you an undesirable hand, rather than blame everyone else, take a minute to learn from it.

Conquer that and your relationships will follow suit.

My final piece of advice, not that I'm technically qualified to solicit it, is to take a long look inside of yourself. Get past the vanity demon that tells you you're perfect and encourages you to take perpetual selfies all day. Go beyond the impenetrable wall that you've built around all your insecurities and dig below the deep crust that's grown around your common sense. There you will uncover your true identity, your true inner asshole or inner crazy. Figure out where you land on the scale and then seek to find someone compatible to your level.

If you're not happy with where you currently reside on the scale, maybe you can find God. And if God doesn't want you, maybe you can quit drinking, start a diet or invest in a yoga retreat somewhere reclusive to realign your chakras. Odds are if you're old enough to read this, cover to cover, it's too late for you. You are probably past the point of no return. Embrace who your experience has made you. If you're batshit crazy, find a man who likes to fix things. If you're a cheating asshole, find a woman with multiple personality disorder. There's someone for everyone out there.

And hey, when all else fails, take it from me, the biggest asshole I know, if you can't beat 'em, you might as well join 'em.

ACKNOWLEDGMENTS

I would like to personally thank all of the people in my life who have had to listen to me drunkenly bitch, whine and blather on and on about this book for the last three and a half years. I'm sorry but I cannot give you back the countless hours you have spent not listening to me, just know that I love each one of you for your terribly divided attention. Though I do feel I would be a complete douche not to mention the real heroes of my neurosis: Mel Neale, Matt Granger, the fine folks at Barney's who never seemed bothered by my entitlement to the corner seat at the bar, the ever-reliable Jack Daniel's, and my cat, Blanche Devereaux.

I would also like to personally apologize to everyone who's ever had the misfortune of dating me. Without those experiences this story would have never come to fruition and the literary world would probably be a better place.

About the Author

Jordan West was born in Northern Ontario in the dead of winter, which basically explains her innate anger towards menial things. In 1996, her family relocated to Vancouver Island because the pain of Tupac Shakur's death was too much to handle. Jordan has written counter-culture columns for a number of publications, all of which were eaten alive by the age of technology. Fed up with gratuitous Facebook posting and free favors for musician friends, she decided to spend her life savings writing this book. Jordan currently resides in Vancouver, Canada in a relatively affordable, rent-controlled apartment on the West Side with her asshole cat and Siamese fighting fish that was last seen two weeks ago.

Manufactured by Amazon.ca
Acheson, AB

14320759R00120